MW00332758

THE TRIUMPH OF THE MAN WHO ACTS

THE TRIUMPH OF THE MAN WHO ACTS

BY

EDWARD EARLE PURINTON

Author of "Efficient Living," etc.

NEW YORK

ROBERT M. McBRIDE & COMPANY

1916

The Triumph of the Man Who Acts

copyright © 2020 Triumph Book Press, *All Rights Reserved.*

For information address **Triumph Book Press**

1761 N Young Circle, Ste 3-180, Hollywood, FL 33020.

First Triumph Book Press hardcover edition October, 2020

Originally published October, 1916

For information about special discounts for bulk purchases, please contact

publisher@triumphbookpress.com | (888) 722-0399

Disclaimer: Information in this book is NOT intended as medical advice, or for use as diagnosis or treatment of a health problem, or as a substitute for consulting a licensed medical professional. The contents and information in this book are for informational use only and are not intended to be a substitute for professional medical advice, diagnosis, or treatment. Always seek the advice of your physician or other qualified health provider for medical conditions. Never disregard professional medical advice or delay in seeking it because of something you read in this book.

1   3   5   7   9   10   8   6   4   2

Discovered and manufactured in the United States of America

www.TriumphBookPress.com

Available in these formats:

978-1-7352897-0-0 (Paperback)

978-1-7352897-1-7 (Hardcover)

978-1-7352897-2-4 (Ebook)

Library of Congress Control Number: 2020942693

Cover Design: -Leslie-

Illustrations: bobservations

Publisher's Cataloging-in-Publication Data

Names: Purinton, Edward Earle, 1878-1943, author.
Title: The triumph of the man who acts / Edward Earle Purinton.
Description: "Originally published in 1916" -- from title page. | Hollywood, FL: Triumph Book Press, 2020.
Identifiers: LCCN: 2020942693 | ISBN: 978-1-7352897-1-7 (Hardcover) | 978-1-7352897-0-0 (pbk.) | 978-1-7352897-2-4 (ebook)
Subjects: LCSH Conduct of life. | Success. | Self-actualization (Psychology) | Motivation (Psychology) | BISAC SELF-HELP / Personal Growth / Success | BODY, MIND & SPIRIT / Inspiration & Personal Growth
Classification: LCC BJ1611 .P95 2020 | DDC 131/.3--dc23

Dedicated to

Chanie - my partner in triumph

CONTENTS

FOREWORD

Rabbi Zusha's eyes flowed with tears. His disciples gathered around his
deathbed to console their great master as his time was near. One said, "Rebbe,
you are as wise as Moses and as kind and generous as Abraham. Surely you
will be judged favorably in Heaven." With trembling lips, Reb Zusha declared:
"When I get to Heaven, I will not be asked why I didn't measure up to Moses,
or Abraham. Rather they will demand: Zusha, why weren't you like Zusha?
Why didn't you attain your highest potential?!"

Rabbi Meshulam Zusha of Anipoli, 1718-1800

———≈———

In a search for triumph, I discovered this book. Through this
discovery, I found my lion.

Although I'm too loud to be mistaken for a bookworm, I have
always loved to read. Growing up in a house where piles of books
bedecked every room taught me their value, especially the older
ones. My parents and all nine of their children love books. My
dad, a schoolteacher for over 40 years, carries a library around in
his head. My mom, an expert on Jewish American history, spends

more time in the 1860s than anyone else I know. Following the path of my five older brothers, I went to a rabbinical college and became a rabbi.

Balancing the responsibilities of being a rabbi was a struggle. The studying, teaching, and schmoozing I enjoyed thoroughly. The other duties — organizing, scheduling, fundraising, and administrating — I found challenging, and ultimately this tipped me off the pedestal of the pulpit and onto the hard beat of phone-sales. There I learned the harsh discipline and grit required to provide stability and prosperity for my family.

Flash forward five years; life is flying along at a synchronous pace and rhythm. My wife had just given birth to our son — a great addition to our growing family — just as we moved into our newly renovated house and settled into our lovely community.

Then the reports started coming in from China. The change that followed brought everything to a standstill. The shakeup that came next was universally felt and experienced; it forced us to redefine and reimagine our expectations and very limits.

Considering my options, I initially welcomed the pause. Sometimes it feels good to slow down. But, after a while, I grew restless and found the abrupt halt to my routine left me gasping for purpose. I determined that I would "hit it big" during this shutdown. I was so sure that I had learned everything I needed to shoot for the moon. Shifting into gear, I splashed around, trying to accomplish too much with nothing to show. In short, I was full of it. After I rapidly developed a series of internet marketing strategies that seemed to be going nowhere, perhaps due to my tensity (p. 87), that, like a drill, was on point but just boring a hole. It took its toll on me, and I fell into a deep depression.

Despondent and in bed for days without eating, I took to writing to provide some relief. I needed triumph and penned the words, "you are a lion, feed yourself triumph" as a motivational mantra. It worked: I absorbed it, believed it to be true, and slowly found my way up and out of bed. Looking for inspiration, I googled that phrase and cracked open a time capsule of American literary brilliance.

Edward Earle Purinton originally published *The Triumph of the Man Who Acts* in October 1916. I stumbled upon a digital copy on Google Books. This book rings out like a bell of clarity from a century passed; its substance and style compelled me to keep reading. I had discovered an author with a wit the equal of Mark Twain's, self-improvement courses that dwarfed Dale Carnegie's and wisdom akin to Ralph Waldo Emerson's. *The Triumph of the Man Who Acts* is a timeless and universal book.

Purinton was also infinitely practical. As I read his advice on how to maximize efficiency, health, happiness, personal relationships, and business relationships, I realized that the powerful, philosophical, and practical self-help systems and tools he presented were the best that I had ever read by an American author.

Failing to find a copy of *The Triumph of the Man Who Acts* in print, I began to research the book's author, Edward Earle Purinton (April 24, 1878 — July 10, 1943). How could a writer of such magnitude vanish, with all but a trace of his works remaining? My mind ignited: his works must be republished.

"Earle," as he was known to his family, inherited from his father an incessantly active mind and from his mother a frail body. After graduating in 1899 from Denison University, he traveled the world in search of treatments for the various mental and health conditions that vexed him for the first twenty-five years of his life. "Some fifteen forms of constitutional disease took turns troubling me; until family, friends and physicians began to despair of the outcome" (*Personal prologue, The Philosophy of Fasting*).

Purinton studied over 500 systems of health, psychology, philosophy, efficiency and healed his many infirmities in the process. He then moved to the Bronx and launched the Efficiency Publishing Company in 1904, headquartered in the Woolworth Building in New York City. With the eloquence of a preacher and the practicality of a shrewd businessman, Purinton set about educating the growing industries and multitudes on efficiency and productivity. He penned articles and essays on business and personal efficiency exclusively for the *Independent Magazine*, a weekly publication circulated in New York City between 1848 and 1928. He served as director of the Independent's Efficiency Service and ran his own consulting firm. Full-page advertisements that promoted his Efficiency Publishing Company appeared in many publications in his day, including the *New York Times*. According to promotions in the *Independent Magazine*, over 10 million copies of his various books and service manuals were printed and distributed in twenty countries. In fact, within the first few months of publishing *The Triumph of the Man Who Acts*, he had already sold more than 700,000 copies! That Purinton's methods and philosophies worked is indisputable. He guided large businesses and manufacturers on how to organize and operate their plants and factories for optimal efficiency.

Insightful and practical, Purinton employs a straightforward, four-fold approach emphasizing productivity, balance, motivation, and the courage to act. To enhance your productivity, he urges, "Nothing stays good unless you try to make it better. And the way to succeed is to regard yourself not an artisan, but an artist! Whether you run a railroad or a typewriter, there is a better way of doing it" (p. 17). He also offers specific systems and practices to "Stop the little leaks, of time, thought, money, vitality" so that you can "accomplish more, with less fatigue" (p. 21). On achieving balance, he states, "Roughly, we may classify all our troubles into four groups: Those pertaining to the body, the heart, the mind, and the soul. Oftentimes they overlap, sometimes they affect the entire being, but always the physical, emotional, mental and spiritual distinctions remain" (p. 112). "First, study out the cause in yourself; second, choose from the many prescriptions offered by authorities the one that your judgment indicates will do the work" (p. 114). On motivation, he writes, "The motor of a man is the motive in him. You can draw a toy engine by a string, but there are no strings on the train that makes a mile a minute — this engine carries its own fire" (p. 16). Purinton suggests, "try this experiment: The next time you feel a conviction, inspiration or desire that seems unusual or even untenable — act on it, fully, promptly and implicitly" (p. 7).

Purinton acknowledges that most of us are afraid to act, fretful about the consequences of doing the wrong thing. He encourages the reader to take a singular approach: "Failure, contrary to the general opinion, is not mere lack of success. Failure is a disease. And the first help toward cure is elimination" (p. 55). He defines optimism as "A firm conviction that everything is coming right, *backed by a firm resolution* to work your head off in that direction" (p. 23). To develop courage, he suggests that you turn everything you do into a system of action so that even if you are idling, you do so by choice!

The Triumph of the Man Who Acts has awakened my inner lion. In republishing this book, I bring forth the shiny optimism and vision of a man who endeavored to live his entire life fully. Purinton's work is purely American in its openness, practicality, and optimism, representing the country's highest ideals. I have begun following the advice he lays out in this book, and it has been transformational. Every day I look to exercise my body, heart, mind, and soul. I exercise outdoors daily, rain or shine. My heart is exercised through the focus and attention that I now give my family. My mind is exercised by trying new things or new ways to do old things. And my soul is exercised daily in prayer, study, and meditation as he aided my return to the teachings and writings of my rabbis and sages.

Just imagine what change can happen in your life when this book reveals the treasures within you.

ARI BERKOWITZ

Morgantown, WV
July 3, 2020

A GUIDE TO THE MODERN READER

Prepare to think. Prepare to engage. Prepare to learn. Prepare to change.

This guide is designed to maximize the benefit of this book to you, the modern reader. It does so by providing context and guidance. I address context through a discussion of the historical and cultural moment in which it was written. I provide guidance in two ways: through suggestions on how to approach his language for improved readability and comprehension and practical advice on how to approach each section of the book for maximum benefit.

Although Purinton's language and style are dated, the substance of his works still carries enormous weight, and you will no doubt find it greatly beneficial. Toward that end, I have reorganized the chapters into five sections: Productivity, Health, Happiness, Relationships, and Freedom. I have also included illustrations to keep you entertained and engaged. Some chapters that were irrelevant and potentially disturbing for the modern reader I kept out of the reprint.

Because some of the language and themes are dated, they may cause offense to the modern reader: you! Knowing that, please keep an open mind as you read this book and focus on the merits of the author rather than the limitations of language, which are a reflection of his era. In republishing this book, my aim is to restore the past, rather than topple it. Please allow Purinton to draw you in and help you think. For example, because this book was written at a time before women occupied the public sphere, it is directed to men. However, everyone, will greatly benefit from his work.

This book was originally published in 1916. You will find that Purinton, like most authors, expressed his views and opinions on current events. It was quite a tumultuous time in America. Industry was roaring, with tremendous reforms sweeping across many sectors, as the country advanced from the Industrial Revolution to the Machine Age. German saboteurs infiltrated New Jersey and blew up munitions depots, filling the air with certainty that America would join the Great War. Strikes sprang up everywhere as anarchy descended. The 1918 flu pandemic wreaked havoc upon everyone.

The tumult of 1916-1920 parallels our own, current chaos. Purinton advised and guided his readers on controlling their internal turmoil, thereby enabling them to flourish and not get caught up in the external noise. He counseled that the status quo would always be shifting; the question is whether you are balanced enough to handle it. Perhaps no era in human history experienced greater change than his. Consider that there was no electricity at the time of his birth in 1878 and that by the time of his death in 1943, progress was being made in computer science!

PRODUCTIVITY

As an efficiency master, Purinton lays out very specific and useful guides to reorganize your life and seize control. He asserts, "when you dominate your day's work, guided by impulsion instead of compulsion, the whole scheme of life changes — you are master, and Fate is your slave" (p. 25). Through detailed systems of concentration, talent focus, and skill acquisition, Purinton lays out a bulletproof plan of success.

An integral part of being productive is knowing oneself. As you work through this section, take a notepad and write down what *moves* you and *motivates* you. Write down your *greatest strength* and your *biggest weakness*. Productivity is doing what you do best, to the best of your abilities. Efficiency is getting the maximum output for your efforts. Once you figure out who you are and what you can do, put that into action and strengthen yourself through slow, methodical exercise. Do this until you can perform your set task to maximum efficiency.

HEALTH

Purinton's discussion of health is particularly effective because he writes of his own experience as a sick child and adolescent who restored himself to good health. "Many a man doomed to die has outlived his doctor, first by *willing* to have health, then by *working* to secure it" (p. 4). How often do we fill ourselves with substances hoping to heal us, rather than *substance?* His chapters on health focus primarily on healthy eating, maintaining a healthy sleep schedule, proper physical exercise, personal hygiene, fresh air, and sunshine.

There is always a way to improve one's quality of life, and self-discipline is the cornerstone. Set for yourself a fixed bedtime; Purinton recommends 10:00 p.m. Drink plenty of water. Eat to satisfy hunger rather than appetite.

HAPPINESS

Thanks to Purinton's efficient work on his health, he maintained an incredibly happy and optimistic outlook on life. Cheerful and insightful, Purinton could dazzle a crowd with his wit and eloquence: "Happiness is a power — not a possession. It is the capacity of being what we are, doing what we can, trusting in what we aspire to — and letting Providence take care of the rest....Happiness is not a gift, but a reward of merit" (p. 106). "Cultivate a healthy sense of humor" (p. 124). Joy and happiness are a state of mind. When you cultivate inner peace, joy and happiness follow. Trying new things and being open to new experiences invites happiness inside. Study the chapters on happiness daily, recognizing that it is personal and unique.

RELATIONSHIPS

Although Purinton never married, he offers sage advice on love and relationships: "True love promises nothing yet performs all. The only guarantee that a lover asks is to be allowed to love, more and better. From the cradle to the grave, we are finding ourselves just as we are learning our need and capacity for love. For as we love, we create; and as we create, we are like God. Would you die for someone? Can you live for someone? Do you belong to someone?" (p. 182).

Purinton teaches that by loving yourself unconditionally, you are then able to invest unconditional love and attention to those closest to you and achieve the ideal relationships. Think of love flowing outward from yourself to those closest to you and expanding beyond. The greater the blaze of self-love, the more you share. Learn from these chapters how to see yourself for what you are, and what benefit you can offer those around you.

FREEDOM

Purinton notes that there is no greater attainment than freedom: "What is freedom? … Freedom is the conscious power to express any, all, or none of yourself when you will, as you will, because you will. This, you observe, is the opposite of license. Freedom means expansion, expansion means exercise, exercise means skill, skill means work — and how few of those who rant freedom are willing to work!" (p. 186). To attain freedom, Purinton recommends that you be willing to liberate yourself. To break out of the prisons of self-doubt, fear, and sadness. To recognize and accept all that transpires, as an opportunity for growth and liberation. The section on freedom will open your mind and release your inhibitions. To let yourself be free, simply turn the pages as you would a key.

This book will guide you to the best possible version of yourself, and allow you to see the benefits and qualities of those around you. Can you picture a life with more energy, focus, compassion, kindness, generosity, growth, wisdom, and efficiency? All of that is possible if you learn to train your mind as diligently as you exercise your body, heart, and soul.

"If you have done all these things, and whatever else occurs in the doing, then look for a chance to help somebody who is down…For the sad and poor and helpless can most appreciate, and will most bless, the prompt and generous nature of The Man Who Acts."

(p. 13)

I. PRODUCTIVITY

"TWO PILLS A DAY SHOULD FIX IT."

CHAPTER 1

The Triumph of the Man Who Acts

THIS is the day of the man who acts.

The world wants him, well knowing that he is bound to forge ahead and achieve what compels rightful admiration.

We respect a man because he has taken what we had, or acquired what we haven't. We respect the man who acts because he displays *control over crises*. This spells opportunity, this makes history, this creates destiny. For to see what should be done — then do it on the instant, caring nothing for appearance, precedent or preachment, is the common mark of the great of all time.

The man who acts possesses courage, promptness, faith, quick-wittedness, farsightedness, a huge will, a holy zeal, and the power to mass his forces on a set point at a set time for a set purpose. Such traits are rare, worth money, and a meed of praise. They command the rewards of the world, they summon the gifts of the gods. If any boon to you be lacking, see why it goes to the man who acts.

Health attends the man who acts, Wisdom guides him, Hope frees him, Joy helps him, Power moves him, Progress marks him, Fame follows him, Wealth rewards him, Love chooses him, Fate obeys him, God blesses him, Immortality crowns him.

Health attends the man who acts. Loss of health is, first, loss of initiative. Disease attacks inert bodies. Germs feed on dead tissue. Every sick man has begun to die; and conversely, no man thoroughly alive can be sick. To be energized from head to foot — body, brain, heart and soul — is to be radio-active and hence immune. Never blame or fear a germ — typhoid, rheumatic, catarrhal or tubercular — blame your own negligence, fear your own ignorance, and make friends with the germs so they will do their work more eagerly. If a house-holder left a pile of garbage in his dining-room, then were driven to despair by rats and flies, who would pity him? We should say to him, "You are lazy, shameless and reckless — clean up or go to jail!" Yet we pity the invalid — who also has garbage in his dining-room or elsewhere in his body — and we say to him, "The way to be well is to fill, up on more poison from the drug store!" When pills are used for pillars, health is bound to topple.

The finest remedy in the world is for a sick man to realize that *he himself must do something*. He must eat less and exercise more; learn to breathe to the bottom of his lungs; find what water will do for him inside and out; smash the fripperies and follies of custom and expediency; understand what life means and get a real object for living; cultivate faith in himself and his fellows; work and play all over; study the birds and the trees and the stars, and be as frank and free as they — in short, get down to first principles, back to Nature, on to Destiny, up to God. Nothing is "incurable" save lack of courage. Many a man doomed to die has outlived his doctor, first by *willing* to have health, then by *working* to secure it. For perfect health is only a by-product of efficiency; whoever does things and delights in the doing thereby

[4]

unconsciously grows deep-chested, lithe-limbed, red-blooded, stout-hearted, clear-eyed, strong-nerved, calm-visaged, clean-souled.

Wisdom guides the man who acts. No book contains wisdom. A book merely echoes what a man learned by doing things. Hence most of our pedagogues are busily engaged telling the young how to follow echoes. The crime in popular education lies in regarding the mind as a memory-box instead of as a motor. The only hopeless fool is a highly educated fool. Many a "fool" who knew nothing but dared all became the world's idol. You see we begin to have real education only as we long and dare to plan and execute our own adventures in life. What if we err? We have been honest. What if we suffer? We have been bold. What if we come to disaster? We have chosen the path of our heart, and though our possessions vanish, our principles rise immortal.

No man has mounted the first step to achievement who has not learned to make mistakes nobly and retrieve them gracefully. The child walks by trusting his muscles despite his falls. The man wins by trusting his aspirations, desires and hopes despite his failures. Civilization throttles instinct, doubts intuition, denies inspiration, attempting to substitute logic or policy or mob-rule for the deeper, higher, finer voices of the soul. Not by heeding the warnings of timid friends or the mutterings of rabid enemies but by forgetting, and if need be defying, the words and habits of others, choosing to heed the inner voices and follow to the end, do we grow apace in wisdom.

Hope frees the man who acts. The chick is a timorous bird, the eagle a valiant. Why? Because the eagle knows the strength of his wings, by his action he overcomes his fear; whereas the chick, feeling his wings helpless, merely squawks and flutters at the approach of danger. Most men, and the vast majority of women, have had their wings clipped. Freedom in action they know not, hence they fear. What do they fear? Poverty, illness, enmity, old age, solitude, night, sorrow, unpopularity — countless things that lie in the shadows of ignorance and indolence. Fear is but chronic inability to act. And what we fear, we invite. If the business of being a desperado were as moral as it is hygienic, we might all profit by a course in brigandage. No man fears himself; hence the way to rout fear is to be oneself so thoroughly and constantly that no outer shadow may intrude. Fears are the centipedes and lizards of the mind, hopes are the butterflies and larks. Hopes lead when we do as impulse or inspiration prompts; fears haunt as we lie prone. When a man despairs call him a drone. At least that will anger him — and ire gets action!

Joy helps the man who acts. The pessimist is always a theorist — never a practical man. From the nagging housewife, lacking system, love and tact, to the magazine "muckraker," lacking a job and envious of men with good ones, the preacher of woe is always a person with an unsolved problem. But to the earnest and the energetic, life is a splendid game; and he who knows the game and "plays fair" is always expecting a victory. Men and women need to limber up; they are too dignified, too conventional, too timid, too expressionless, too unreal — and too rheumatic. A little boy in mischief is always contented. We may not like the mischief, but the action of him is ideal, also the courage that defies a rule-of-thumb. And in mature life, the youngest, cheeriest, soundest man is he who always delves in something new. A destiny, like a diamond, is a matter of digging. Happiness lies at the heart of some herculean task. And the mere act of stretching our mental and spiritual muscles creates a physical buoyancy, to thrill and impel and renew us. Woe is merely a blind wish of a weakling. The lion, fettered and bound in his cage, presents a sorry countenance; the lion, speeding from his lair to the open, grapples with his foe and mightily exults in life.

Power moves the man who acts. From the new science of experimental psychology we learn that the average man uses only a small fraction — a third to a tenth — of his inherent brain-power. The rest lies dormant. Why? Because *original* thought is lacking, and that is the only kind that really builds the cells of the brain. Now original thought and independent action are closely related. All discoveries and inventions, all great commercial undertakings, all humane projects and philanthropic institutions, were the outcome of the brain of a man who had a new idea, recognized its value, became absorbed in it, worked it out for himself, and by proving it challenged the world's attention. The human brain is an electric battery, Universal Spirit the power house, and personal ambition the set of wires on which the current runs. Seldom is the battery connected aright, with the source of power above, or with the channels of power in human life. Great deeds are the product of great desires. And most human beings are so trivial, so unattractive, so commonplace, because whatever desires they had in childhood have been crushed in the world's routine of repression, monotony and apathy.

Try this experiment: The next time you feel a conviction, inspiration or desire that seems unusual or even untenable — *act* on it, fully, promptly and implicitly. If the result seems a mistake, never mind — a new channel of power will have been opened in your brain, and as you grow familiar with this, you will be astonished at the increase in efficiency.

Progress marks the man who acts. One of the popular fallacies of the day is that we can grow healthy, wealthy, happy or great by merely thinking ourselves so. Does an artist need only a frame? The artist of character or achievement may well choose the right frame of mind — but to create the picture, he must toil hard and long. The worst cases of failure, mental, moral and financial, that the writer has ever seen were those of habitual, professional thinkers and dreamers who scorned the busy life of the world, imagining themselves beyond the need of exertion. A definite plan of action, and a determined execution of that plan, must underlie all permanent advancement. History is peace where prophecy was action. The whole aviation art and industry is based on the unremitting efforts of two plain men — the Wright brothers, who kept trying while others merely talked. Schwab, the greatest mechanical genius of the steel trade, liked his work so much that he preferred it to play. Ask any captain of the world's progress what brought him where he is — he will say, "I did more than was expected of me."

Fame follows the man who acts. Not that fame is desirable — it is rather most uncomfortable. But to those who have not outgrown the small-boy habit of wanting to carve their names on the scenery, this is an argument for action. Study the names of the famous men of the present time — Edison, Marconi, Roosevelt, Kipling, Burbank. Each of these can do, has done, some one thing better than anybody else. They were not content to be idle while things could be improved. They are great because they kept going in spite of great discouragements. Fame is but the echo of a man's determination. Only those remain obscure who did not take a strong enough vow.

Wealth rewards the man who acts. The fortunes of the plutocratic families — The Astors, Rothschilds, Rockefellers and Cecil Rhodes — were founded on the action of a man who first saw and filled a great public need. Money is the measure of what people want; but they have to be shown before they know what they want. They did not know they wanted the telephone, telegraph, sewing-machine or automobile — until somebody foresaw the demand and prepared to meet it while his neighbors slept. Somewhere, in the acquiring of every great fortune, a man took his future in his hands and stepped off into space. Somewhere, also, he came back to earth so completely that his method, his machinery, his regularity, surpassed that of his rivals no less than his dream outshone theirs. Both in imagination and in execution the builder of riches displays a lordly stride.

Love chooses the man who acts. The question will be, not "Is the girl a beauty, a social queen, and a deft caterer to man's conceit?"

but rather "Is the man a worthy specimen, physically, mentally and morally; will he make a true husband and a good father?" The right marriage-dower is not coin for the woman — it is character for the man. So, when women legislate, the dower-customs will be changed. Such a revolution will be hard for the ousted lords of creation to accept. The way to prepare for it is to do things, morally and spiritually, as eagerly and effectively as they have always done with brute strength. For the woman always yields to strength in the man. Even the poet — wan, soft thing — has a power of imagery that the millionaire must acquire if he keeps all of his lady's heart. The matinee idol and the soldier on parade maintain a semblance of action. This is what endears them to feminine worshipers. Would you win your lady's adoration? Do something, anything, that no other man she knows could or would do. For every woman's king must be a conqueror.

Fate obeys the man who acts. Luck is a myth. Chance plays no part in success. Whoever looks on a leader with envy merely looks at him with ignorance. For every man who attains supremacy of any kind has done something to earn it. Paderewski was born musical — yet so were thousands of others. What made Paderewski the world's greatest pianist was the habit he had of playing a note or phrase until he got it right — often three hundred times at a stretch. Edison was born with a gift for mechanics; but his matchless wizardry is only his capacity for work, he can go for weeks on half the food and sleep that his helpers demand. Beethoven, meeting deafness, went on writing music in his mind. Milton, stricken with blindness, learned to see with his soul. Napoleon, weak and sickly, grew healthy by growing lion-hearted. All these men did things, either using a good heritage or overcoming a poor one, to an extent beyond the zeal or courage of the many. Each act, each word, each thought of our life to-day becomes a mosaic in the mansion of our destiny. Thus we decree our fate to ourselves.

God blesses the man who acts. God is Light and Light is energy. God is Love and Love is power. Thus vitality is the backbone of virtue, and no man can be good who is lazy. The great religious leaders have called themselves most blest of God. And they were all men of action — Luther, Calvin, Savonarola, Spurgeon, Moody, Mott. God even prospers "bad" men who use their brains and bodies to effect. Their sins are punished, but equally their talents are rewarded. Why are the churches losing ground, why are false sects springing up? Because the churches have as a rule wasted their finest energies and opportunities in talking. If clergymen had waked up fifty years ago, as they are now doing in the glorious effort called the Men and Religion Forward Movement, they would not now be apprehensive of Christian Science, New Thought, Mysticism, Socialism, or any other cult that really aims to supply what the church failed to consider. In theology, the doctrines are dying, because bereft of deeds. A zealous Buddhist is a better Christian than a lukewarm Baptist. And there comes a time, in the growth of every soul, when he regards weakness more unpardonable than wickedness. For sin is generally blind, while indifference knows well its own guilt. Honest effort, just that and nothing more, builds our estate in Heaven. So the ignorant, the poor, the afflicted, the oppressed, have a better chance to be exalted hereafter, because they are forced by harsh necessity to exert themselves.

Immortality crowns the man who acts. The royal insignia of Albert of Belgium gave him no crown among the immortals; but the royal stature of his soul, as revealed to the world in his glorious defense of his people under fire, has now been writ in gold for the eyes of generations unborn. When before, in all recorded time, did the world's geniuses render a fellow-mortal such a tribute as the Book of King Albert? Whether it be Joan of Arc burning on her pyre, or a common soldier bleeding in the trenches, they who risk their lives for the cause they love are illumined by the fame that shall be as light forever. The world is full of heroes, whom perhaps only the angels sing. But of all those whom the world honors finally, each one has taken a superhuman risk, and so achieved a superhuman task. This alone repays for the ills and hurts and heartbreaks of life; and this alone makes one immortal.

Suppose now that a man wished more of the health, wisdom, joy, power and progress of action, how might we suggest that he energize himself for greater efficiency? By starting right now, to put a few simple things into operation, letting their cumulative force renew and reconstruct his life. So our answer would be this:

Stop talking — learn to speak only as you and your friends will somehow profit thereby.

Stop worrying — when you can handle the present as well as God will handle the future, you will laugh at your worries.

Stop wishing — a wish is confession of weakness. Want what you want hard enough to get it, or else feel superior to the need.

Stop criticizing — only an ass wastes energy in braying.

Stop hesitating — it is the plunger who goes to the bottom of things. And whether gold or mud is at the bottom, the man who has found it rests.

Stop imitating — a real ruby is worth more than an artificial diamond.

Stop idling — either work; or play, or sleep, or travel; in short, make even your rest-period a thing of ambition, volition, system.

Stop hurrying — when you teach your brain to outrun your body your body will stay quiet.

Sit up straight, walk with your chest out, look every man in the eye and declare yourself as good as the best. Humility is not hump-shoulderedness.

Go to the open window and take a dozen huge breaths, deeply and slowly, stretching your legs and arms at the same time, and feeling the purified blood leap through your veins and arteries. Do this whenever you have a headache or a grouch.

Read books that build — not the mush in the six "best sellers." Goethe, Shelley, Browning, Emerson, Whitman, Darwin, Epictetus, Kant — these men produced food for the minds of real men. And of all literature of action, biography is best — you can judge the progress of your neighbor on the achievement-path by the heroes whose lives he studies.

Eliminate idlers from your acquaintance. This includes all who enjoy play more than work.

Lose yourself in your work. Come early and stay late. Use every spare moment in developing methods first to work better and then faster. If there is a man higher up in the same business, devote an evening a week to studying how he got there.

Analyze your average day, and find how many hours a week you waste. Then consider that your time outside of working hours is worth twice as much — because that belongs to you, while the other is only your employer's. Thus, if you earn ten dollars a day, every hour outside the office routine is worth at least three dollars — too much to squander.

Line your walls with portraits of the world's conquerors, starting with Napoleon and Lincoln, finishing with the greatest man in your own special field. Traits of character map themselves on the face. The countenance of a winning pioneer is of itself a heaven-born stimulus.

Picture yourself in absolute command of the place you aspire to, in permanent possession of the thing you want, with every ambition satisfied and every aspiration met. Failure is a fool's name for lack of grit; not being a fool, you will not talk of failure.

Face to the front, unceasingly and unqualifiedly. Consider that the past never was, excepting in the lessons it has brought. No man regrets while still he marches on.

Attack the hardest job in sight. Do this first. A little reflection will show what it is — probably a slipshod habit or ugly propensity or chronic weakness that needs handling without gloves. The man of might is he who was merciless to himself.

If you have done all these things, and whatever else occurs in the doing, then look for a chance to help somebody who is down, lift a burden that has grown too heavy, whisper a word of love and sympathy to the lonely, the forlorn, the misunderstood. For the sad and poor and helpless can most appreciate, and will most bless, the prompt and generous nature of The Man Who Acts.

CHAPTER 2

Daily Guide to Success

EVERY human mind is a miniature of Niagara.

The latent power it contains is huge, tireless, resistless.

Most minds, however, merely seethe, froth and rumble — *they have not yet been electrified!*

When we establish in our mind the electric plant of *self-knowledge and self-will*, we find we have the power to guide and move great communities, and to increase our value to ourselves a hundredfold. As Niagara is now, so shall we be when we utilize all our mental force.

The business of the writer, during the past twelve years, has been to rouse human minds and bodies into new health by new action under new stimulus. He has trebled his own efficiency, he has seen others treble theirs. The following paragraphs suggest various means whereby average minds have been electrified and made to yield unsuspected energy.

I. GENERAL PRINCIPLES OF MIND-EFFICIENCY

Why do you work at all?

That is the first thing to settle in your mind, before your mind can gain power.

In any field of labor, whether finance or philosophy, music or surgery, mining or aviation, the big men are made big *by their motive.* And conversely, the small men are kept small by *their* motive.

The motor of a man is the motive in him. You can draw a toy engine by a string; but there are no strings on the train that makes a mile a minute — this engine carries its own fire. Every inefficient man is being pulled along by some child's toy string, that has no connection with his mental machinery. But when a man starts to generate his own fire — then look out! An express train is coming.

What string moves you? Is it habit, or fear, or necessity, or greed, or cowardice, or people's opinion? If any such force keeps you at work, you have never grown up. And you will always be a joke to strong men — as a boy's play-engine is a joke to people who want to get somewhere.

There are three motives underlying, and impelling, good work

1. The enjoyment of the work itself.

2. Some kind of service rendered by means of it.

3. A great personal ambition ahead of it.

Unless you love your business or profession, or unless because of it you can help some one dear to you, or unless it leads to a splendid future for you — you would better stop here; without a new motive you can never be efficient. But if you want to find a new motive, to energize and speed you on, this book may help you do it.

The only unfortunate thing about work is to regard it unfortunate. If you think it a curse, it will curse you; if you think it a blessing, it will bless you. Therefore —

1. *Look at your work as a wonderful opportunity.* Measure it not by the pay you get, but by the power you gain. Your employer, whether Fate or a man, gives you two salaries when you wake up; — first the pay-envelope, second a blank cheque on the Bank of Fame for you to make out in the sum you desire. And the cash means less than the collateral. You can tell a big man from a little one by the way they view a dollar-sign ($); the big man climbs on the straight part, the little man loafs on the crooked. Until you can see over and beyond the money you get in return for work, you are likely to get no more money, and sure to get no opportunity. I would rather live on $5 a week and have a chore-boy's job in a place with unlimited advancement a possibility, than take $50 a week in a Government position with my future guaranteed permanent — permanent because dead. Your true income is your outlook.

2. *Believe yourself the best man in your line that ever lived.* Of course you aren't — but you *may be.* And maybees put their honey on the branches of the faith-tree. I do not boast my family tree, because I have an idea that small, fresh apples are better than large, dried ones. If you ever ate dried-apple pie, you know how to feel when a man starts to get proud of his family, his business or his reputation *merely because it is established.* Nothing stays good unless you try to make it better. And the way to succeed is to regard yourself not an artisan, but an artist! Whether you run a railroad or a typewriter, there is a better way of doing it. The best, of anything, was never yet discovered. Immortality is but an inkling of the best, only by improving everlastingly do we grow immortal. Work is a fascinating game when we treat it as a puzzle whose solution is perfection.

3. *But be sure you are in the right work.* My college chum is wearing out his life in an insane asylum. He was a born manipulator of men, with a taste for the big game of human seeking. Before he knew himself, he studied medicine and became a doctor. He was never happy, and finally his reason fled. He was meant, not to write prescriptions, but to rule empires! Many a bright youth is maddened by something the size of pills, when he craves the huge risks and rewards of life. A school, a business, or a household, that fails to teach and practice Vocational Training is offering the shell of education without the kernel. There are leaders of wide repute who are now endeavoring to banish the "square pegs" from the "round holes." Consult one of these authorities if you are in doubt as to your choice of vocation.

4. *Learn to enjoy your work, whatever it is.* When people who don't like olives eat enough olives, they generally come to like olives. A good way to start liking distasteful work is to make yourself "eat it up," as the slang goes. No man likes his own laziness, and the fellow who dawdles is bound to be disgusted with himself. Hence the grouchiness of the time-server. Good yeast can make any bread light — the shape or color of the pan doesn't matter. Just so, good ambition can make any work light — the size or complexion of the job doesn't matter. Nearly every great man has fought his way through a long, painful, ugly, mean period of drudgery. But he had a light in his eye, a fire in his heart, and a force to his "punch," that made his foes quail and his obstacles vanish. Whatever a man is forced to do against his will contains some great lesson that Providence knows he must learn. When the fault is corrected, the weakness overcome, the impediment in himself removed — lo, the hard and uncongenial task disappears!

5. *Find and trust your supreme desire.* What do you most want to do and be in the world? Have you thought this out? Do it next Sunday,

or some evening this week, or as you ride to and fro in the street-cars. The bird was born to sing, the flower to bloom, the star to shine; the bird sings, the flower blooms, the star shines — and each is healthy, happy, good. Every man was born to do something — some special thing. Doing it, he grows in strength, influence, character. Ignoring or evading it, he dies — in body, mind and soul. What were you born for? What are you aiming for? What would satisfy you? The first essential to efficiency is a fixed goal.

6. *Plan your future in detail, then join it to your present.* In other words, build an air-castle as lovely as you can, but dig a cellar under it, where to keep a furnace and a sack of potatoes, to warm and feed you while your dream is coming true. The conspicuous failures of the world are of two kinds — the dreamers who have no foothold, and the plodders who have no foresight. Both are inefficient, the one from too much imagination, the other from too little. Imagination must be your architect, but your *builder's* name is Common Sense.

Let us illustrate our meaning. Suppose you are a clerk in a great department store. One of a thousand others, you chafe at the long hours, meager pay, harsh treatment and drear monotony. But suppose you are not one of a thousand others — for you have dreamed a dream! You would like to be an artist, a writer, a traveler, a somebody with a larger, freer, nobler calling. And you mourn that such a hope is doomed, where you are? A hope is never doomed *until discarded.* Wherever you are is the place to start for somewhere higher. Unseen opportunities are lying all around you. Wake up, and get going. You would be an artist? Hoard your pennies, take a night-course in Show Card Writing, ask to letter the placards used daily in the store, think out original designs, be transferred to that department on larger pay, and then climb! You would be a writer? Study advertising, see how to improve your own daily newspaper bulletins, practice writing ads in your spare time, submit them when good enough to your advertising manager, get to be his valued assistant, and cultivate a "style" that will make you a great author if that be your destiny. You would be a traveler? Find how the head buyer got where he is, and emulate him — he enjoys a deal of travel and is well paid besides. You would be an actor or public speaker? Learn how to enunciate better in your "selling talk," how to choose your words, how to impress customers favorably, how to win their patronage and friendship, how to stick in their memory. You would be a corporation president? Study shorthand and typewriting, be private secretary to a famous man, acquire and adminster his methods, then strike out for yourself.

In short, *analyze all avenues of approach* to achievement, then choose one and enter *now*. The principle holds, whatever your work may be, that *intention* makes *attention*, attention sees and forces opportunities. The urchin lazily paddles a raft across a pond, eating an apple or whistling a tune; — he knows nothing of water as a rapid transit medium. But the Oxford oarsman, trained and stripped and eager, plies the water with a scientific stroke and unswerving aim; — he makes water serve his locomotion better than his own legs would do. It is not the stream of our surroundings that directs our fate, it is our choice of boat, and our way of handling it. Great men see, where small men sigh.

7. Having chosen your path, follow it though the skies fall. You can't pick daisies and plow for Destiny at the same time. And every man whom Fate rewards, once walked in a furrow. Suppose that every time the sun shone, the farmer said to himself: "Nice day — let's go fishing!" ... How fast would he get his ten-acre field sowed in wheat? Most people's *minds are fixed on pleasure* — not on progress. Yet all triumph, in the end, is just trudging along. Think of a picnic — and no day is too hot, no basket too heavy, to spoil your fun. Every good plodder has a picnic ahead. And there is no fun like work — when the stakes are high enough to play with a vim! The backbone of Purpose is persistence. To the great opportunity, great obstacles are way-marks; and if we remember this, we shall not faint when we grow tired and discouraged. When a man really starts to get somewhere and do something, everything and everybody seem against him. But it was always so — God had nothing but darkness and dust from which to create orbs of light and worlds of beauty. Neither enmity, sorrow, hunger, pain, poverty, weakness nor misunderstanding can affright you, or move you from your path, while a God-given purpose and strength carries you on. Whether you write an immortal song, or build a new empire of commerce, you will be sustained until the work is done, if that is your work to do.

8. *Stop the little leaks, of time, thought, money, vitality.* If you are in business of any kind, learn the easy way, and short cut; you can accomplish more, with less fatigue, when you have mastered the *psychology* of efficiency. Investigate "Scientific Management," subscribe for magazines on Business Building, apportion a fixed sum and time for your trade books and papers. Do you read the accounts of murders and scandals in the newspapers? Waste of time. Worse — dust and gravel in your mental machinery; it is unwise ever to think of human ills and wrongs, unless we can personally help to correct them. Do you entertain a great deal, hoping to ensure a mammoth circle of friends? More waste of time; — *friends* don't need to be "entertained," and much feasting alienates the gods. Do you play bridge or pinochle incessantly? Waste of brain cells; — the kind of thought that makes a fine card-player would make a fine business man or professional woman, if applied to *real* problems. Do you live in a "classy" neighborhood, for the sole purpose of appearing classy? And to pay your rent, do you skimp on food? Waste of energy; — the efficient man never economizes on food or clothing, he has the best, he knows that his

vim and nerve and endurance largely depend on the quality and quantity of his meals, and that his professional standing requires fresh, clean, elegant, appropriate garb. When you order cream, have cream, not skim-milk; skim-milk feeding gives skim-milk force. Pay enough respect to your personality to wear clothes that suit you, in color, contour, fabric, style.

Such items of thought are good investments of your gray-matter, yielding returns in character, influence, individuality, self-respect. And what about your amusements? Do they refresh you, or exhaust you? A good test of whether you are on the right efficiency track is the query: Do you work in order to play — or play in order to work? The average man *uses* not more than a fifth of his mental power, and *misuses* about fourfifths of what he uses. I'm not very "good at figures," but if my arithmetic is right, you have a chance of being 96 per cent, efficient where you now are 4 per cent. This may be overstated, as the *average* man would never read this book at all. But the gain is sure to be enormous, when you stop all waste of time, energy, money, health, motion and emotion, in order to achieve your goal sooner.

9. *Try to see yourself through the eyes of your critics.* How to have a good education: Go to school to your enemies and rivals. Your foe, or competitor, or critic, has a grappling-hook in your weak spot. Don't strive to flee the hook — strive to mark the spot, and cut it out. Are you a poet? Then avoid the flowing tie, flowing hair, flowing manners, of a poet; — the world hates, not your poetry, but your *pose*. Are you a doctor? Strive to outgrow *false* professional dignity, the look of condescension and air of omniscience. Are you a merchant? Ponder this fact: Eternal hustle makes hash of the mind. Learn to meditate, to relax, to enjoy philosophy, to love music; and, other things being equal, your business will increase. It is not a proof of genius to be jeered at; and to disarm criticism is to hasten conquest. Study the

art of being an individual, without being a freak. Organize a mutual improvement society, in your family or club or place of business; locate the faults, in yourself and your neighbor, that impede efficiency; offer a healthy prize to the one who changes most in a given time; — then go to it!

10. *Be an optimist, first, last, and all the time.* (But keep the fact safely concealed — there is nothing so irritating as a fellow who positively never gets angry, impatient or downhearted. Whenever I see a "smile that won't come off," I feel a wild desire to punch it off. The smile that won't come off belongs to the man that won't get on. The cheer-up brother needs churning down — he foams well but doesn't weigh much. Definition of an optimist: A man who can smile when he sees another optimist.)

What is optimism? A firm conviction that everything is coming right, *backed by a firm resolution* to work your head off in that direction. "All is good?" Yes, but not for a long time, after we have begun living consciously, definitely, wisely, bravely, does this truth show in our circumstances and surroundings. The heedless, the cruel, the selfish, the undeserving, may seem to pass us in the race. But God awards the trophies — and no man guilty of a moral "foul" shall be honored finally, whether he arrived first or last. Worth, like water, reaches its own level. Don't worry about promotion — worry about *preparation.* To earn more is to yearn more, then learn more. Nature abhors a vacuum as much as she ever did. And when a fellow with a half-empty head occupies an eminence that you aspire to, Nature will crowd him out and you in when your head, being fuller of knowledge, shoves his lightweight noddle over the edge of the law of gravity. Let the man above you teach you his merits, but the man below you teach you your mistakes. And remember that doing too much never put a man back — it is the worker who does a lot of tall thinking *outside of working hours* who presently shall run the business. Whatever you do, you are paid to be a first-class machine; only as the man studies, overhauls and repairs the machine when it doesn't have to work, will the efficiency-mark advance.

In a great factory, many workers toil on many parts of the final product. The worker may not know how the result of his thought and skill may help to fit the plan and create the output of the owner and maker. But the end is perfection if only each worker does his share. This world is the factory of God, Maker and Owner of us and our talent. He plans far ahead, leaving us to work out each our own pattern of usefulness, but always keeping a larger place in readiness, *when our part is perfect*. Knowing this, we can do our best — and smile.

II. EFFICIENCY-METHODS FOR THE DAY'S WORK

If a man wishing to cross a congested city street should deliberately turn around and *back* over, what sort of lunatic would he be? And how far would he get, unbumped?

Yet the average man, facing the crowded *events of the day*, shows an attitude of mind and body just as foolish, reckless, fatal. And when they run him down, impairing his health, temper and estate, he blames the "grind of business" or the "cruelty of competition" or the injustice of "blind luck." Every day of modern life is a crucial transition, and the lad who gets across walks through with his eyes open. He does not eat and drink and dress and sleep and think and work and play as *his father* did, or as *his neighbor* does. He makes his habits serve his ambition, his moments all add to his power.

When your job is on top, hammering the life out of you, you can neither see clearly nor toil effectively; but when you *dominate your day's work*, guided by impulsion instead of compulsion, the whole scheme of life changes — you are master, and Fate is your slave. If you will adopt the following schedule, and will stick to it long enough to get results, you will find a new strength, skill, buoyancy, courage, composure, permeating and reconstructing your daily life. Most of our readers live in the city, and do brain-work of some kind. Hence our schedule is made for them. But the *principles* of it apply to anybody, anywhere. And few changes will be needed for your own use.

To produce an effective day's work, you must begin the night before.

Keep your bedroom window wide open, all night, every night, and night and day if possible. If too cold, add more covers. Draw your bed away from the window — dress and undress in a warmer room — but *keep that window open.* There is no other way to prevent the morning dullness, drowsiness, headache and fatigue, which are merely poisoned blood from breathing poisoned air. Those who can't wake in the morning aren't awake to this fact.

Pajamas impede circulation. Wear a nightgown; as light and thin as possible, to let the pores of the skin "breathe" all night; and cut low in the neck to avoid overheating of the back of the brain, which causes restlessness.

Have the best springs and mattress for your bed that money can buy. Perfect rest is a prime factor in abundant energy. And a thin, hard, lumpy mattress, with stiff, scant, noisy springs, will knock your next clay's work galley-west. When you sleep is not the time to be a Spartan; then is the time for solid ease and comfort. Investigate this and equip a new bed if you have to.

Now for the morning of a day of power.

1. When you first wake up, *clean out*. All the body-poisons have been pouring, through the night, into the alimentary canal. You

can no more think and work with those poisons in you than you could start a fire on a grate full of ashes. Rinse the mouth. Drink two glasses of pure, soft, spring water, to flush the stomach and sweep it clean. Have the bowels move — the pint of water, with a little exercise, should effect this, when the new habits have had time to work.

2. Go to the open window and take twenty huge breaths, filling the lungs slowly and gently, but deeply and thoroughly, and holding in mind the thought and purpose of renewing brain and body with ozone and electricity from the fresh, morning air. Hold the breath a moment; while inspiring and retaining it, stretch the arms and legs, tensing all your muscles to the utmost; then as you let the breath out, relax the muscles. If this exercise makes you dizzy, start gradually and put more vim in it as your health improves (vertigo is a vice, it convicts your blood of a lazy, bad character).

Or, take a brisk walk around the room, carrying a heavy weight. Or, exercise with dumb-bells. Or, get a rough Turkish towel and follow your bath with a vigorous rub of the whole body, applying harsh but merry friction till the skin glows.

In short, *get into your muscles* before you get into your clothes. Your brain will be twice as clear, since the worn-out cells of the day's thinking will be renewed twice as fast by the blood that races, after exercise. Gymnastics are a joy — not a task, when you know how. (But if you suffer with any organic trouble, ask your physician's advice before you engage in muscle-building.)

3. Take some kind of cool bath, when you are warm from exercise. It may be a plunge — a shower — a mere dash of water over the body with the bare hands, depending on your nerves and vitality. Then rub quickly dry, and on with your clothes. Taken properly, the morning bath sets your blood tingling, your nerves exulting, your brain working clearly and forcefully. If you don't know how to take

it properly — don't feel warm and keen after it — don't come to revel in it — ask your doctor what's wrong.

4. Eat the lightest breakfast you think you can without starving. A heavy breakfast makes a heavy mind; the blood you want in your brain, to think fast and earn money with, settles in your stomach when food has to be digested. You won't starve with no breakfast at all. The writer stopped the breakfast-habit ten years ago, his general health is now three times as good as then, and he knows hundreds of people who have had the same experience. Above all, don't "eat and run." He who eats and runs, eats and regrets. Food unchewed is undigested. And no brain can be effective with soggy lumps of fermentation in the stomach. When the "boss" has a morning grouch, just pity his poor stomach, and be glad if you can't afford the time and money to load yours up, needlessly.

5. Say little, read little, think and plan much, before going to work. The man who doesn't talk at the breakfast tables knows his job — he is saving thought and energy for grappling with the day's problems. Indeed, the principal function of a morning newspaper is to make a man forget his home troubles before he lands among his business troubles. A happy householder who reads on his way to work hasn't got his brain oiled properly — he should *spend that time in mapping out his day, foreseeing probable events and turning them all to account, establishing faith in himself and his destiny, creating an atmosphere of power, enthusiasm, promptness, cheerfulness, vim and snap and zeal, before he enters the office,* or studio, or shop, or store. Efficiency is born in the first half-hour of the day, or not at all. Get to work always a few minutes before you have to. Be in full swing when the others lazily straggle in. Plan each day so as to achieve some definite advance toward your goal. No man ever held his own who did not reach for more. And the time to read, to converse, to idle and frivol, is *when the day's work is done*, not before. Be cross, if you have to — but concentrate in the morning.

6. Arrange your work if possible so that intellectual phases of it come in the morning, mechanical in the afternoon. Normally, the brain is clearest and strongest in the early hours of the day, when sleep has refreshed it and nothing has occurred to vex the emotions and irritate the nerves. Therefore do your planning in the morning, receive then your important visitors, discuss then your serious problems, leaving the routine side of things, demanding mere execution, for the afternoon. And, from the beginning of the day, get and hold an upright posture, that your lungs may have full play. How are you sitting or standing now? Chest way out and up, abdomen way in? Pull yourself together, lift your chest mightily, breathe toward a point as high as your eyes, and *imagine* your lungs rising till they touch it. Science proves that power comes more from breath than from food. Learn how.

7. Drink a pint or more of pure, soft water, some time during the day. As the engine must have oil, the body must have water. It is needed for digestion, assimilation, circulation, respiration, elimination.

8. Eat an *efficiency lunch* — not a haphazard table d'hote dinner, at the noon hour. Maximum nutrition, minimum digestion, is the watchword. There is nothing more basic to efficiency than the right kind, amount, preparation and consumption of food. Violation of this rule means a drowsy, "dopey," do-less afternoon. Get a book on Diet and learn to feed yourself as rationally as you would feed your horse. And take your time at your luncheon; eat less and enjoy more; the stars won't fall if the waiter is a minute late, nor the worlds collide if your neighbor gets his first; a little rest and quiet before and after eating is fundamental to good digestion; so bottle up your haste, can your unripe temper, and let the meal proceed with joy overflowing. If possible, read quietly, or walk slowly, or just sit and ruminate, a quarter of an hour before going back to work.

9. Insert a 15-minute rest-period in the middle of the afternoon. Certain great factories have demonstrated that a recess about three o'clock, devoted to music or ball-playing or dancing or reading, makes the worker so much fresher and stronger for the remaining two or three hours that the extra things accomplished more than make up for the time occupied in relaxation. If you can arrange this, do so, with a part of the time spent in slow, deep, rhythmic breathing. At least change from one kind of work to another, giving a new set of muscles and brain-cells their share of exercise. In this connection, observe the wisdom of acquiring the art of complete relaxation. You can learn to let your muscles go, feel your nerves loosen, close your eyes, make your body sink as a dead weight, stop even your brain from thinking, and get the *good* of sleep, while sitting upright in your chair, or in the noisy, jerky, street-car.

10. When your day's work is done, forget it. Work is weakness when carried home. Say to yourself when you close your desk: "There is no such thing on earth as business; the rest of the day belongs to me and my family; so any thought of my mercenary job that follows me home will get bounced as a pestilent fellow; culture, friendship and pleasure now claim me till the silence of night takes possession; and work is no more till the morrow." In short, learn to loaf with your whole mind and body, no less than to work that way. Romp with the kiddies. Chase the dog around the house. Get a punching-bag and make believe it's the fellow who said you wouldn't succeed. Limber up, and to-morrow you'll shake down more golden apples. Dress for dinner — if only to change your collar and tie. Wear a smile to the table, and pass it around. Eat a good, large, old-fashioned dinner, enjoying every morsel, heeding not the sad prophecies of pale food-reformers, but making your good lean, stomach perform lustily. Having eaten no full meal since last night, you deserve one. Spend an hour on it. Make a rule that any one who gossips or grumbles or

scowls or hurries at the table has to pay some forfeit to the crowd. If perchance you eat in a boarding-house, do something rash to break up the lugubrious silence and arctic atmosphere (mayhap engendered by the astute landlady to hasten dyspepsia and lessen the drain on the larder). We are fed by thought as much as by food. And a gloomy dining-room forecasts the tomb.

After dinner, enjoy yourself. But if you are a genius, like Edison, and your workshop is your playroom, our advice to "forget work" will be suddenly overlooked. Any man whose efficiency is very great, won it by superhuman sacrifice. So your recreation will be tempered by your hope to be a winner in your work.

If you spend the evening at home, loosen up the tight clothing — collar, corset, belt or suspenders, and give your blood a chance to circulate. In your home, you can learn to approximate the Grecian costume — sandals and a single loose robe; in so doing you will more nearly approach the buoyant health, strong body and keen brain of the ancient Greek. Many physicians now advise the daily "air-bath," as a means of quieting the nerves, toning the blood, assisting the heart, lungs and stomach. The skin grows hungry for air as the stomach grows hungry for food. And as a preparation for sound, refreshing sleep, nothing excels the habit of exposing the unclad body to the gentle current of pure air in a room with a wide-open window. But avoid feeling cold; start gradually, letting the body quicken by degrees.

It has been said that the great men of New York were great before they came to the city, or else grew great because they leave it. New York is a physical babel and a psychic boiler-factory. We are deafened by it — harried — confused. We cannot hear ourselves until we get away. The first cause of inefficiency is lack of inspiration. The men who forge ahead have got hold of a new idea. But new ideas are as welcome in the average New York office as lilies in a sawmill. They cut you up here, and make of you something they can sell — or they shove you to the discard.

What is the remedy? Don't forsake your ideas, but *follow them up.* Get to where you are free to apply them; hold onto them with a viselike grip until you are there; and remember that the mold of every business "machine" was a mind that dared be original. The goal of success is reached by two horses driven abreast — *originality and opportunity.* Don't kill the first mental steed — harness him to the second.

What is the application? Just this. *Night is the nestor of new ideas,* and to be much alone when the world is dark and still means to gain quick solution for your problem, fresh impetus for your advance, overwhelming power for your next day's work. Many a famous man knows that he must wait, to think and plan wisely, for the silence and solitude of night. In the city we forget the stars; but in their light we discern the great truths of our existence — to which the city flare and flame blind us. To have poise, foresight, mental grasp, reserve power, omit an occasional theater party and walk till midnight in a park or suburb of the city, revolving in your mind your heart's chief desire and praying to be shown the way to reach it best. Every mighty man is something of a mystic. And to mount his highest pinnacle of yearning and faith, he now and then shuts out the world. Every leader, from Napoleon down, plunged headlong into work with resistless momentum because he came from a vast height of his own imagination. Dream yourself in command of your world, dare to follow the dream's lofty bidding, then seize and grip that job of yours with a zest and vigor strong enough to shake the planet. Work is effective just so far as a great want leads it, and a greater will drives it. See that your work is led and driven properly.

CHAPTER 3

The Boon of Concentration

TO every one of the boons of life, the short cut is concentration.
No matter what the goal ahead of us may be, the first step
is to find and follow the path of concentration. Out of the blind
thicket of human destiny, that surrounds, tangles and impedes the
great majority of us, the one clear, open, swift way to freedom is the
path of concentration.

What do you need most? Health — money — power — leisure
— friends — counselors — advantages — opportunities? Learn to
concentrate, and whatever you need most will come to you. The
law never fails.

I am not talking metaphysics. Indeed my first duty is to rescue the
word *concentration* from the mouths of metaphysicians. Nowadays
nearly every city in America has a fluttering bevy of selfstyled metaphysical teachers who would, for a suitable honorarium, induce you
to "practise concentration" by sitting vague and vapid in a "concentration class," or fixing a rapt gaze on a crystal ball, or doing some

other fancy exhibition stunt. This brand of concentration is not the one I am writing about.

Suppose you are riding east, on a New Jersey road, fifty miles out of New York. You meet a man walking west. He is gaunt, begrimed, unshaven, unwashed. He hobbles on a twisted cane. His clothes are torn. He looks the picture of hunger, friendlessness and woe.

You are moved with pity. You stop and ask him, "Why so forlorn?" He answers, "I have no friends, no money and no food." You ask him, "Where are you going?" He answers, "I don't know." You ask him, "Why did you leave the city?" He answers, "I forget the reason just now." You ask him, "How long are you going on like this?" He answers, "Till I drop from weariness or fall ill — then some one may give me a lift." What do you do? You buy the man a meal, ring up the police station, have him taken to the psychopathic ward of the nearest hospital, and try to locate his relatives and friends.

On the road of destiny the average man is walking west. In the mental geography on the map of his mind, he is aimless and power-less as a ragged, starving tramp. He hobbles on a twisted cane of tradition, habit or misinformation. He hasn't enough mental food to keep him nourished — and most of what he has wouldn't pass a pure food inspector. He follows a rut of routine, looking neither ahead nor above. His psychic raiment is mud and tatters. His moral expression is meaningless, like that of a man with a wandering mind. He does not know where he is going, or why he is going anywhere. He is waiting for some one to give him a lift — or send him to a hospital. Why all this vacuity, poverty, tragedy, in the life journey of the average man? *Loss of the power, loss of the path, of concentration.*

Is the picture overdrawn? From reading thousands of letters, by men like this, I say it is not. Four persons out of five that you meet are mentally and spiritually lost. They have never found themselves, nor their place and work in life. Lacking a goal, they lack the grit and gumption that a man with a goal has to get. Their actions, thoughts and emotions are at loose ends — kite tails flying in the breeze. A man's career is but the measure of his concentration.

Let us define our word. Concentration is the science of knowing what we want most to do, have and be; the art of achieving it; and the habit of forgetting it.

The prime essential is a fixed goal. A good example here is the racing crew of a big eastern university. Every member of the crew knows just where he must end the race and land the boat; he has learned to time his stroke to the fraction of a second; he has stripped away every ounce of superfluous clothing — he has for weeks lived on simple fare selected by science; he has fully mastered the principles and methods of team work.

Just where am I going to be at the end of the race of life — or five, or ten, or twenty years from now? Have I a definite picture of the goal in my mind? Have I chosen, and proved, the shortest, easiest and best way to that goal? Am I working every day, every hour, with this in view? Are all the useless things left behind? Is every act in working hours properly, regularly timed, so that my daily output is sure to equal my maximum? Do all my habits of life speed me on to my goal — or do some of them handicap me? Is every one of my working associates eager to help me win? If not, why not — and where am I now? Have I advanced all that was possible? Have others advanced more? Do I know the causes of my slowness in progressing? How shall I remove the obstacles, in my surroundings and myself? These are a few of the questions for every alert man or woman to face bravely and settle fairly, as initial steps on the road of concentration.

Before one attempts to concentrate, he should have his greatest, finest, strongest desire shape and designate the exact goal that he would reach through concentration. Then he should line up his present system of work, thought, and home life with his ultimate goal, to such an extent that he can see how every move he takes puts him forward. Then he should make his will a power so firm, prompt, resistless, that he does precisely and fully whatever he sets out to do. Then, he is prepared to learn to concentrate. A difficult program? Surely, and gladly. What are we here for if not to face hard jobs with a smile? What keeps a man small is the habit of looking for easy things.

There is, however, a shorter, easier way. Few people have learned how to plan, foresee, and lay out their lives, from here and now to the larger place ahead. It will suffice, temporarily, to learn to concentrate by doing our daily work — whatever it is, more thoroughly, quickly, easily, and thoughtfully. Suppose, for example, you are a stenographer. Your first concentration exercise will be to make every letter, manuscript and memorandum *perfect* — so as not to waste a moment of your chief's time in the location and correction of your mistakes. When you have made every piece of work faultless during a whole day, try it for two days — three days — a week. Having attained a perfect record for a week, you can then focus on speed. Without losing in accuracy, you should be able to gain perhaps thirty per cent in rapidity, merely by ceaseless practise in mental and manual concentration. There are new books and systems to aid you here. Find them, and study them. Your next object will naturally be an easier way of doing the work you have made better and faster. Modifications of scientific management, and service departments of the large typewriter companies, should save you needless motions and responsibilities. Then you may begin to *think for your company*, especially in relation to your desk and departments, for increasing the sales and decreasing the costs. Now if you are an ordinary stenographer, you have never practised any of these four kinds of concentration exercise — that is why you remain an ordinary stenographer. Promotion follows concentration.

All great men are masters of concentration. And any man will be great when he has learned to be master of concentration. The texture of the brain counts for little. The size of the brain counts for less; the *use* of the brain is the measure of human power. Concentration is merely intensive farming of the mind; and what the scientific farmer can do for and with his crops, the scientific thinker can do for and with his thoughts. We have to-day the new agriculture, we shall have to-morrow the new menticulture. The barren mind, as the barren field, is merely one that has not been cultivated. And the output of any mind, as of any field, can be doubled by the right methods of cultivation.

A number of books now available discuss the metaphysical side of concentration more or less truthfully and impressively. But the majority of these neglect the practical side. Out of perhaps fifty fundamental factors in the science and art of concentration, I would here dwell briefly on ten of the most important. If you incorporate only these ten in your daily habit of thought, work and life, you should eventually double your power of mind — and your productivity, happiness and usefulness.

1. *A focus of taste and talent.* Always concentrate on something you want to do, and may reasonably hope to do well in course of time. There is a group of things, different but related, which every man or woman could perform with unusual skill when trained and experienced. Learn your vocational group of inherent possibilities, and confine to this group your exercises in concentration. The prime focus of our will should be our work; and our work, to succeed, must literally be ourselves. It is not true, as we are told by certain peddlers of metaphysics, that we can always be what we mean to be. It is true that we can be what we were meant to be! The first move in concentration is to find what we were meant to be.

2. *A clear, firm and useful ambition, both ultimate and immediate.* Have you learned how to use mental photography? The world's most powerful camera is the human mind; a picture of our desired

achievement there scientifically produced will outlive and outreach a hundred photographs of our face by a mechanical instrument. The purpose of concentration is creation; therefore we must know exactly what we want to create, what motive is back of it, what use ahead of it. To concentrate without a present object is to cheat your client or employer; to concentrate without a future object is to cheat yourself. Haphazard work is the universal bane, whether in commerce, education or religion.

3. *A surplus of energy, and control of the sources of vitality.* The mind that creates must be a self-renewing dynamo of impelling, animating, electrifying thought. Physical health is the basis. Whether you put your whole self into your brain and evolve a masterpiece of music or invention, or whether you put your whole self into your fingers and weave a rare fabric or weld a steel frame of a thirty-story building, your power of concentration depends on how healthy you are. Get a physique, or your mind will crack under the strain of prolonged, intense concentration, which to a master worker ends in exhaustion. You must eat and bathe and exercise and sleep with vitality in view. You can't live an ordinary life and do extraordinary work. Have you developed a satisfactory system of creating and conserving your maximum of energy?

4. *A regular concentration habit, both mental and manual.* When you lie in bed a few weeks, you can hardly walk. To walk right, you must walk every day. So, to think right, you must think every day; and toward a given point, as you walk. If a man started for the post-office, then decided to go to church, then got a notion to visit the blacksmith shop, and finally went home without reaching anywhere, you would call him feeble-minded. Yet the whole thought-world is a realm of wandering minds — we merely do not see them wander. Can you think so hard on a plan or purpose or piece of work that you forget to eat and sleep, don't know whether it is today, yesterday

or tomorrow, and feel concern about nothing in the universe but the all-absorbing thing you are doing? If you can, you are on the road to somewhere; if you can't, you are a mental and moral idler, with an empty future like your empty past.

Learn to spend at least a half-hour each day fostering and strengthening your life purpose, by a period of intense, original, constructive thought on the best and quickest ways of reaching your goal. And form the habit of doing *everything* promptly, thoroughly, scientifically. When I throw a fistful of discarded papers at the wastebasket, and the wad fails to hit, I get up and walk over and place the consignment where it belongs. Not to be neat, bless your heart — a man too neat is an unmanly mixture of ladylikeness and nothingness; but rather to keep in trim the wholesome habit of hitting what I aim for.

5. *A proper observance of time and place.* For concentration of mind the best time seems the early morning, when brain is clearest, body strongest. And the best place is wherever you can be in silence and solitude. Great thoughts are crushed by the crowd. But for concentration of *body*, the turmoil of business competition seems required — in their manual skill men are naturally gregarious.

6. *A punctilious regard to the physiology of thought.* The brain is mostly blood. Hence a copious and ready supply of rich, pure blood is the first essential to powerful thought. Do not try to concentrate when physically tired, or less than two hours after a full meal. Give brain and nerve foods a large place in your diet. Learn to think at home in a bathrobe and sandals — every bit of tight clothing serves to congest the blood and retard its passage to the brain. Consider also the matter of posture; lie flat if that helps you to think hard.

7. *A systematic study of practical psychology.* A thinker must know the mind as an electrical engineer knows the dynamo, not for the sake of the theoretical knowledge, but so as to get the greatest service out of the mechanism.

8. *A balanced life.* The strain of holding the mind on a tension must be offset by frequent periods of absolute relaxation; with such aids to carefreeness as music, a romp with the children, a bit of gardening, or a long tramp. The ordinary man must learn to be a firebrand — the extraordinary man must learn to be a vegetable. Kindly, however, do not try to be a vegetable until you know you are a firebrand, as the supply of human vegetables now gluts the market.

9. *A dauntless perseverance.* You may need forty years to work out your life purpose. What of it? The holding of the purpose makes you strong, and that is really the mission of the purpose. Ten thousand obstacles may hinder you. No matter — the fiends plague and fates besiege only the man of power. You are stronger than they, as soon as you know you are. Even your old friends may turn from you, misunderstand you, join against you, as you fare on and up. Keep smiling — new and better friends are waiting. Everything you try to do may seem to go wrong, and whelm you in failure — only that you may learn to survive success through learning to survive failure.

10. *A never-failing fund of optimism.* The road of concentration, as you may have surmized, is not necessarily a boulevard of roses. But the real people travel here, and the real rewards lie ahead on this road. Besides, this road gets easier and easier, while the road of inertia gets harder and harder. A man doesn't know what life is for till he tries to do something his neighbors say can't be done. Concentration is the science of removing the word "can't" from the mind. When this has been performed — this necessary operation on the intellect — such a new array of opportunities will be manifest that no pessimist can live in their presence. Accordingly we say: Become an optimist now, that you may feel at home with the triumphant workers when they gather at the goal of their ambitions. Only the optimist sees opportunities. And the road of concentration is the world's highway of opportunities.

EFFICIENCY CONCENTRATION TEST

FOR ANY MAN OR WOMAN BETWEEN 15 AND 55 YEARS OF AGE

DIRECTIONS. Read first this article. If any point is not clear, talk it over with some friend who is a logical, deep thinker. On the basis of the article, interpret and answer the following questions. Where the answer is Yes, write numeral 10 in blank space on the right line. Where the answer is No, leave space between I and 10 expressing degree of assurance. Don't favor yourself — make each numeral too low rather than too high. Add column of numerals for your percentage in concentration, so far as the test goes. On this test, the grade of a really big man or woman would be perhaps eighty per cent., while that of the average person might be not more than twenty-five per cent. If your grade, honestly reckoned, is 40 or 50 per cent., you are probably ahead of the majority, but still far behind the leaders.

1. Have you a great ultimate achievement, based on your talents, clearly pictured in mind for ten or twenty years hence? _____

2. Do you know how to work toward your goal, and is every day's work put minutely in line with your advancement? _____

3. Have you a surplus of energy, so that you are never tired, vexed or despondent? _____

4. Can you think or work so hard, five hours at a stretch, that you forget to eat or sleep or answer the door-bell? _____

5. Do you spend at least a half hour every day in planning your future, studying your work, and improving yourself? _____

6. Is your earning capacity regularly increasing at a substantial rate? _____

7. Have you read at least two modern books on the principles and methods of concentration? _____

8. Have you learned how to make use of all the functions of your mind? _____

9. Do you always tackle the hardest job first, and choose hard jobs in preference to easy ones? _____

10. Are you so sure of final success that nothing and nobody can discourage you; and when everything seems to go wrong, you calmly forge ahead with even greater strength and determination? _____

_____

Total equals your approximate grade in the knowledge and use of concentration.

CHAPTER 4

The Efficient Optimist

THE first idea to be drilled into the mind, heart, soul and body of every human being is the firm assurance:

> *"You Can!"*

These two words are the biggest in the language. Everybody needs to hear them told, powerfully and often. They should be engraved and illumined above the door of every home, school, church, hospital, factory, forge and shop in America.

The greatest favor to be rendered any man is to tell him how much he can do, and how best he may do it. This is the problem of health, of labor, of marriage, of education, or religion, of culture, of character. And Optimism offers the solution.

The power of the Universe is locked in every human mind. Our first duty is to find, release and use this power. Great men are great only because they have explored and revealed their own minds. They have achieved this, without exception, because of their conviction that they could do some one thing supremely well.

Great men are always optimists. They believe in themselves, their work, their mission, their destiny. Even such orotund pessimists as Carlyle, Schopenhauer and Nietzsche were incorrigible optimists as to their own wiseness.

There is a science of optimism — and it is not safe to be an optimist until you have learned the science. If you are a natural optimist, born that way, you should at once denaturize yourself by marrying a pessimist, or taking one as partner, or hiring one as personal adviser. The reason for such precaution lies in the fact that a natural optimist is generally a natural fool.

Because of this deplorable fact, I have little use for merely hereditary optimists. Like poets, they should be heard and not seen. To see one is to become violently discouraged as to the future of the race. To make any man a pessimist, shut him up in the house with an optimist.

There are depths of anxiety, perplexity, want, despair, along the road that every one must travel who aims at a far, high goal. Not to evade these, but to emerge with strength renewed, hope established and sympathy enlarged, is the ideal for an optimist who deserves the name. Convictions are the only sure foundations for ambitions. And to follow your convictions means, often, hell. The test of your faith is how long you can stand on it against the world.

Many people have a notion that an optimist is a cheerful, happy-go-lucky sort of person, empty of cares, burdens or problems, smooth and sleek and well fed, favored of gods and men. Believe it not! All the real optimists I know have been through battles, worries, woes, privations, that would tear the heart out of an ordinary man a hundred times over. Not the man who always smiles is the optimist, but the man who can always turn frowns and tears into smiles! The consciousness that everything must finally come right is not born in a moment; we must first consciously do the thing we know to be right, thousands of times, and must watch ourselves gain a step of ground each time, before we can form the habit of trusting the Tightness of the cosmic plan. The days of blind faith are over, the days of intelligent action are here. An efficient optimist hopes entirely without reason, but works entirely with it.

Analyze the requisites for your own work and thus command your own future. Doubtless you possess a longing, dream or wish to have, do or be some particular thing worth while. Are you a blind and lazy pessimist, fearful of yourself and too weak to look your own wish in the face? Are you a superficial optimist, drunk with your dream and hoping in a vague way that some kind fairy will waft you by magic to the Land of Heart's Desire? Or are you a scientific optimist, hoping with your heart while planning with your head and working with your hands?

Every position of trust to which we aspire will demand certain specific traits and forces — mental, physical and moral. To learn what these will be, then to acquire them, is the initial step to scientific advancement. To become an optimist one must know how he can advance; to remain an optimist, one must know he is advancing. We enjoy only what we have earned. Our habits of earning depend most on where and how and why we toil. Hence, in laying the foundation for a lifelong optimism, one of the first moves is to consult the leaders in our chosen trade or profession, and to organize the physical, mental and spiritual forces in ourselves that the leaders in our field think necessary.

A thing done well is never done easily. What place do you want to reach — what price are you willing to pay? The place is always there for him who gives the price. How much do we want a thing? Enough to work for it, wait for it, weep and starve and bleed for it, give up the world for it, go through despair for it? Then we shall have it. And until then, if it is a boon worth having, we should not be able to use it.

How does optimism aid efficiency? By renewing, refreshing, sustaining and strengthening our bodily physique, mental constitution, moral character and psychic reserve. The path to any great success is lined with many small failures; and the assurance of ultimate success lies in the perception to see and the power to use the lessons from these failures and to go higher because of them. This perception and this power come only to the optimist.

The world was against Newton when he proclaimed the law of gravitation; against Harvey when he discovered the circulation of the blood; against Wagner when he wrote his epics of harmony; against Franklin when he searched the skies for the secret of electricity; against Darwin when he announced the law of evolution; against Bell when he made the first telephone; against the Wrights when they labored on the airship; against Burbank when he dared to invent new species of plants and flowers; against Froebel when he taught how to understand children better. These men all had to create in themselves an optimism strong enough to carry them through and beyond the world's ignorance, blindness, inertness, fear, hate, opposition. And the law still holds. The greater your work and the finer your message, the more you will be antagonized. Your only safeguard is in scientific optimism.

What does scientific optimism do for the human machine? It promotes good digestion and a corresponding sense of buoyancy and cheer; it straightens the backbone, physical and moral; it assures deep breathing and the liberation of more energy; it favors sound sleep and repose at all times; it lends force, clearness and alertness to the brain because of a purer blood stream and a surer life purpose; it empowers the will by enlargement and establishment of one's faith;

it steadies the nerves for a calm, firm handling of the crises, problems and duties of everyday life; it provides the key to a storehouse of moral dynamics, available only when we see, think, believe and hope for the best; it expands our influence and makes hosts of friends; it opens communication with higher, spiritual avenues of original conception and power, by means of which the ordinary man becomes great, and every man a conscious master of himself, his work, and his destiny.

The charm and beauty of optimism is that every one may acquire it. No matter how poor, weak, ill, sad, forlorn we may be, we can all become optimists, and in doing so can finally change the worst conditions into the best. How? For answer, let me state a few of the rules in the science of optimism, by means of which hundreds of pessimists, including myself, were taught to think and act sanely and effectively.

1. Stop grumbling, whining, pining, worrying, pitying yourself. Get busy. Do something, anything, to shake you out of the frozen rut of regret.

2. Look around you and see how much worse off other people are — and how much better they are behaving. Study the lives of the world's heroic figures, then observe how small your troubles are, and surmount them.

3. Find a purpose big enough, and make a will strong enough, to carry you up and over mountains of difficulty.

4. Hold *yourself* entirely responsible, not anything nor anybody else, for the troubles and trials that come upon you. They are the results of your past mistakes, to be borne wisely and bravely; or they are the means to your present development, to be studied calmly and utilized fully. Weeping at misfortune only blinds one to its mission, and blaming something or somebody only weakens one when he should be strongest.

5. Analyze each loss, pain, perplexity or hardship, saying to your-self, "What can this teach me, how can it develop me?" When sorrow ends in strength, sorrow becomes joy.

6. Exercise, work and play out of doors all you can. The muscle of an athlete seldom goes with the mind of a worrier. The pessimist is always a negative person, and the cultivation of physical power tends to cure pessimism. The "blues" leave the brain as red blood pours in.

7. Build up your digestion. Much pessimistic thought is merely auto-intoxication, or a stagnant condition of arteries and nerves due to a lazy liver, weak stomach, or overtaxed kidneys. A man weak in food science is almost sure to be weak in faith.

8. Learn which of your mental faculties are naturally dull or defective, use modern methods to sharpen and strengthen them. A person weak in the faculty of hope, or of caution, or of economy, or of self-esteem, or of continuity, or of any of a dozen more faculties of the mind, will have occasion to grieve much and often; but mostly on account of his own folly.

9. Study books that teach the art of happiness, and the cure of illness, poverty, oppression, sadness, fear, confusion, doubt. The mind needs tonics far more than the body does. And an optimistic writer is doctor, nurse and druggist for an ailing mind. Of course, the Bible is the best manual of optimism ever given to the world. But there are a few modern books that teach the modern science of optimism, in a modern way, to fit modern conditions. Every home, church and school should contain some of these, and every man or woman who hopes to do great things should take such a book for a constant companion.

10. Make yourself smile, whether you feel like it or not. We enjoy looking at our picture because the photographer made us "look pleasant"; and to look pleasant long enough is to feel pleasant. All

tragedy borders on smiles; don't plunge so deep into tragedy, play a little more around the edges. We have millions of years in which to become strong and wise and great; should any happening of a moment rob us of our poise?

11. Don't be ashamed to cry. There are depths of disappointment and grief when nothing but a great flood of tears will sweep the mass of woe from the valleys of our minds, and reveal again the path to the heights.

12. Lift some other fellow's burden — and you will find that your own has fallen off, or at least you carry it more easily. Self-absorption is the root of pessimism; dig out the root and the branch withers. Failures in optimism are always failures in altruism.

Scientific optimism is faith in self, God and man, plus knowledge of material conditions required for the attainment of a specified goal, plus will to work long and hard, and use every means and event, good or ill, for the transmutation of experience into achievement. The lever with which to move the world is an irrepressible faith, grounded on irrefutable knowledge, backed by an irremovable will. Have you this faith, Have you this knowledge? Have you this will?

TEST FOR EFFICIENT OPTIMISM

DIRECTIONS. Write numeral 5 in blank space at right when answer is affirmative. Leave space blank for negative answer. Add column of numerals for your approximate grade in right use of optimism.

1. Is your will unbreakable, your faith invincible? _____

2. Have you learned to give in, without giving up? _____

3. Are you glad to be told of your mistakes? _____

4. Do you rectify all mistakes as far and fast as possible? _____

5. Can you smile at losses, abuses and disappointments — while in the midst of them? _____

6. Do you believe we always get just what we deserve? _____

7. Do you know why you haven't succeeded as fully as you hoped to? _____

8. Can you see how your greatest present trouble can be turned to advantage? _____

9. Could you be happy if all your friends deserted you? _____

10. Are you familiar with at least five books on the nature, acquisition and preservation of optimism? _____

11. Can you name at least five great modern optimists, and show how their optimism adds to their efficiency? _____

12. Have you kept the faith, romance and idealism of your early youth? _____

13. Have you also acquired caution, system, economy, tact, shrewdness, accuracy, patience, responsibility? _____

14. Are you determined to be and do the best there is in your line of work? _____

15. Can you make fun of your own peculiarities, and enjoy a good joke on yourself? _____

16. Have you formed an advisory partnership with a pessimist? _____

17. When you are pessimistic, do you always diagnose yourself and learn what physical or mental weakness is to blame? _____

18. Are you helping to make your friends and neighbors optimists? _____

19. Do you believe in quiet, rather than verbose, optimism? _____

20. Is your final ambition unselfish? _____

_____

Add column of figures and learn how efficient you are as an optimist. (Grade should be at least 90.)

CHAPTER 5

How to Succeed

WE are children not of men but of Destiny.

Hence, real failure is impossible. Every living thing was born to be great, each in its own way. And to achieve greatness can be nothing more than to express what is from the beginning.

The marvel of human life is not the greatness of the few, but the blindness of the many. Whoever sees the truth about himself and lives it, must be great. He cannot escape if he would. To the man in full possession of himself, even genius appears commonplace. Because even genius is uncontrolled.

We are all great.

This consciousness, grounded in the depths of our being, is the rock of truth on which any earthsuccess must be established. Pity the man who ridicules youth's "dream of greatness." The gigantic figures of history have all molded a dream out of star-dust, then taken their stand upon it, and challenged the world to a battle of spiritual musketry. Planets are insignificant before the onset of the man whose dream has become determination.

Of every great man this one thing can be said: *He is himself.* No matter what that self is, to be it is to succeed.

What great men felt, they have been. What they saw, they have done. What they wanted, they have lived for, worked for, waited for, dared hope for. You, or I, or anybody, will succeed by grasping the law under which all men succeed. Wherein we fail, we have simply broken the law.

Success is the power of using one's self as Nature intended. Success is not a definite object to be gained or point to be reached; those who look upon success in this way never succeed. The measure of success is expansion of individuality. If to-day we can do or be or understand more than we could yesterday, we are succeeding. But the rewards, such as money, friendship, or fame, are purely incidental. And that is why we can never judge of a man's happiness by his apparent success. Only he is permanently happy who is consciously growing stronger, day by day. And whether he lives in a hut or a palace matters little.

Human power flows through many channels; to succeed is merely to find and use the one that belongs to us.

Success is fundamental to Happiness. To be thoroughly happy, we must have, or have the power to have, many things. In these latter days of metaphysical mummery, you perchance have been led to suppose that Happiness resides in a rose-water expression, alabaster attitude, and general feeling of no-account-ness. Believe it not. The first ingredient of Happiness is *grit*, simon pure grit. And the man who has never been forced into battle is hiding like a coward in a borrowed dream of bliss.

We are part animal, part human, part god. Corresponding to these three natures in one, the temple of Happiness has three portals:

those of *Wanting, Getting,* and *Forgetting.* The first is the door of the animal, the second that of the human, the third that of the god. The outer court is *evolution,* the inner court is *adaptation,* the shrine is *transmutation.* We cannot reach the divine state except by wanting something violently, getting it by conquest, then using it for a higher purpose than we first had. In short, Desire is forerunner of Deity. And the Oriental preachment of slaying Desire is equivalent to shutting God out. Being good by being indolent is like running an electric road by stopping the current at the switch.

Here is an idea for all men: If you would be really happy, cultivate the mother in you. It is the selfish, brutish, clumsy, blind, and coarse manpride that crushes the flowerlike things which if allowed to grow would bloom into Happiness. No man is complete until he pities himself for being a man.

It is as natural for a human life to succeed as it is for the lark to sing, the rose to bloom, or the bee to make honey. The vast number of human failures, partial or total, may serve to prove the distortion, repression and artificiality of what we call civilization. The great successes of the world are the souls who would not let themselves be interfered with. The first move toward achievement is to become self-centered.

Clip the wings of the lark, and the song dies; chill the heart of the rose, and the bloom withers; threaten, deny, and discourage the little unfolding child, and another half-man staggers into the ranks of the millions of half-men, blindly, sullenly, fighting for bread. To succeed is, primarily, to be educated from within, out.

Failure, contrary to the general opinion, is not mere lack of success. Failure is a disease. And the first help toward cure is elimination. Unwholesome food in the body is the principal source of disease; unwholesome thought in the mind is the principal source of failure. Every man who falls short of his own desire has a wrong idea somewhere in the back of his head. This wrong idea paralyzes effort, vitiates hope, renders the sufferer, inactive, morose, pessimistic. Find what it is, get it out, put a healthy one in its place; that is the way to succeed.

A few unhealthy ideas are these.

A spirit of rebellion. This prevails in those who imagine success due to external gifts. "Others have a better chance, a finer education, a larger talent, a luckier fate; therefore they succeed." Emphatically not; chance, fate, good or bad luck, accident, fortune, or misfortune, are myths invented by the weak and cowardly to hide their own shortcomings. Napoleon, Lincoln, most of the world's great spirits, made capital out of hardship and opportunity from limitation. Success, primarily, is a valiant refusal to be downed. We need a lot of healthy discouragements to put our fighting blood in condition. Rebel? Yes, at our inefficiency. The only righteous anger is that provoked by our own weakness.

A habit of fault-finding. The way to cure unpleasant things is to ignore them. Yet there are men to whom the universe lapses into chaos for a day because their eggs were scrambled wrong for breakfast; and there are women who see the sun awry when a ridiculous tirly-wirly on a newly made gown slides out of plumb by the fraction of an inch. A mind absorbed in trifles cannot even understand the cosmic force which enlivens those that achieve. Nothing matters, utterly and everlastingly. Get that fixed — then big things will commence to happen.

A feeling of self-complacency. They say that "all is good." Ultimately, yes. But if you perceive the finer meanings of life, you will be torn with a huge discontent and forced to break through the sodden crust of misunderstanding that keeps the souls of men apart. Ages of effort, infinities of power, could not make of this world what it should be. And for any man to be satisfied with what he has done, or had, or been, is for an ant to boast of a hillock of sand in the shadow of the Himalayas.

A tendency to impatience. The earnest and ambitious are as over-anxious as their sluggish brethren are indifferent. But consider how the masters of the world toil, plan and wait for their object of endeavor. Poise gives power.

A confusion of desires. Do you know just what you want most? If you don't you aren't living; you are merely vegetating. In every life there is, originally, one supreme desire. Uncover it, focus on it, make it your duty, joy, and religion. Then you will see God. It is the divine fire of a consuming purpose that justifies and glorifies creation. Would you melt away the doubts and cares and worries of routine existence? Then dare to burn with fervor until the veils of compromise part and fall to earth.

A dread of solitude. Isolation is the birthplace of great ideas. And great ideas, grown, become great achievements. I think the most colossal figure of history is that of Napoleon guarding his lonely watch-fire while the world slept, and in his mind sweeping opposition off the globe. The world never wakes until the man who has been aloof returns with his vision. Be much alone, think to yourself, look far ahead, partake of the Infinite, and grasp human destiny in the hollow of your hand.

To the cells of the brain, erroneous thought is actual, virulent poison. It destroys or impairs nerve tissue with unfailing potency. In addition to the foregoing pathological ideas or habits, we may note the following: Envy, anger, idleness, irregularity, overserious-ness, flippancy, dependence, self-indulgence, pride, egotism, fatalism, fear of public opinion, ancestor worship, imitativeness, greed, hate, a mixed motive. These all invalidate success, which is but a normal, healthy state of mind in action.

To cure the ills of the body, we administer a large increase of pure air, food, and water.

To cure failure, a disease of the mind, we suggest the following wholesome, invigorating thoughts:

1. *Get a reason for living.* Most people have lost theirs. And with the reason, vanished the joy. Vision some one thing you are going to do or be; then hold to that purpose though the skies fall. A fixed aim is the backbone of spirituality, without it the moral nature collapses.

2. *Study the lives of the great.* Not because they lived, but because they are living. Men make history, history unmakes men. Read biography — not history. Note the insurmountable obstacles that great men plowed through — then dismiss your pet sorrow with a long farewell. Best friends are not relatives or acquaintances; rather will they be found in the pages of a book that grips the heart. The lives of the pioneers are the richest heritage provided for human sustenance.

3. *Esteem all conditions good.* Ultimately they are. And to see just how, we have only to look far enough ahead. Attain the vision of Robert Browning, and you must love the world as he loved it.

4. *Be positive.* Gritting the teeth, compressing the lips, or stamping the foot, is a fine spiritual exercise. If you lack the nerve to strike out from the shoulder, take boxing lessons. One of the current fallacies of the day is the delusion that spinelessness accompanies a high state of unfoldment. God gets things done.

5. *Eliminate the non-essentials.* Including pink-teas, gossip-parties, fashion promenades, polite conversation, duty correspondence, society calls, four-fork etiquette, senseless bric-a-brac, and heirloom junk. About one thing accomplished out of twenty is useful; banish the other nineteen.

6. *Oxygenize your worries.* Most readers are natural-born thinkers. That means more blood in the brain than ought to go there. Consequence: a dire plight of auto-intoxication which many take for profundity. Play something and get jolly; run around the house a dozen times when night has fallen and respectable folks are nursing the fire; enroll in a gymnasium and learn something worth knowing; dance a jig, or start a pillow-fight, or belabor a punching bag; make vigorous exercise a habit of second nature, and achievement will come a great deal faster.

7. *Develop imagination.* The men who forge ahead are those who can see without their eyes. And every notable deed was fully pictured in the mind before it could be given outer shape. A constructive ideality is the ground-plan of material progress.

8. *Make improvement your watchword.* The top is always reserved for the best. What one does matters not, if he does it better than the other fellow. Unhappy conditions are intended to strengthen happifying qualities. And failure is impossible while one keeps trying.

9. *Cherish one friend.* There is nothing so empowering as to be understood. In our hearts, the wisest of us are just little babies, wanting to be mothered, and loved, and praised for being good. If we have some one to share ideals with, we can never be lonely or despairing. It pays to cultivate such a friend.

10. *Establish connection with the Overbrooding Spirit.* By way of prayer, song, meditation, sacrifice, poetry, or any other avenue to the Larger Life, let the real advance be toward heightened consciousness and broadened sympathies. What we gain is but the answer to what we feel. And to be in quivering touch with the vast Divine Purpose is to move things of earth with a force overwhelming. A religious devotion to somebody or something is the motive power for success. They who fail are but disconnected with their Source. Infinite light, infinite energy, infinite joy of living, await every mortal who puts himself in line.

CHAPTER 6

Efficiency Is Service

A NOTED efficiency engineer, who works twelve hours a day and begrudges the time to sleep and eat, was asked the secret of his love for his work. "Efficiency is the science of improved service," he replied, "and the best fun I know is putting a smile on a face that wasn't looking for it." He was right — and the real measure of your efficiency is the number of smiles you can put on the faces of your clients, patrons or customers, also of your clerks, friends and relatives.

"How can I serve you better?" is the question that should dominate the heart and mind of every ambitious man or woman. Greater is he who serves than he who receives; but greatest is he who both serves and receives. To obtain every penny that our time and toil are worth, but to give a graciousness, thoughtfulness and zeal so far above reward that money cannot pay for them; here is the ideal "trade balance" for a nation or an individual.

"Better service for patrons and employees" has come to be the slogan of the world's greatest business concerns. Good service benefits the server more than the served. It cements the served to the server, and makes a transient customer a lifelong friend. I know of numbers of people who do their buying at a certain store because once a clerk or official of that store did them an unexpected, uncalled-for service. Men have joined a church because the minister seemed as anxious to serve them when they hadn't joined as if they had. Young folks have selected a college because some teacher of the college, making a lecture tour, was genuinely kind to them in offering counsel about their education.

TO SERVE BETTER IS TO SAVE MORE

The first reason for efficiency is economy. Well, to serve better is to save more. The officials of one of the wealthiest corporations are so fully convinced of this principle that they have made their watchword "The customer is always right." Even when the customer is wrong, the fault he finds must be rectified to his own satisfaction. The loss of his good-will means more to the concern than the few minutes and dollars which he requires for adjustment of his grievance. Moreover, a grouchy customer often becomes the finest advertiser for the store when his complaint brings full redress; a man feels so almighty good and pleased with himself when the vast machinery of a modern business all whirrs to the tune of his command!

The costliest things are the needless mistakes, and the worst mistake in a trade or profession of the modern world is defective or deficient service. The service of manufacturer to wholesaler, of wholesaler to jobber, of jobber to dealer, of dealer to customer, of employer to employee, of employee to employer; these services, when properly rendered, will increase financial success all down the line. Apart from the spirit of altruism that should control and animate our work, the scientific reason for laying stress on service lies here; that *the man whom we serve is our best critic*. The faults in a clerk are sure to be known to his employer — and those in the employer to the clerk. A good move is to capitalize the custom of criticism, and to render ourselves more effective by stopping the mouths of our critics. We all want to please ourselves, and the quickest way to do it is to learn to please the hard-to-please. Don't ask me how — try it and find out.

I am speaking from experience — painful experience. It sometimes happens that a reader violently disagrees with me. When I was very young, upon the occurrence of such an event I would look down at the intruder and murmur, "How ignorant and coarse the fellow is, really not worth a second thought!" Later, when I acquired enough health to have some fighting blood in my veins, I would shout in my mind at the critic, "You're dead wrong; what you need is to have a hole punched in your head and some sense poured in!" Later yet, after the world had knocked and battered me around sufficiently, I came to look on every critic as a friend; the more he railed, the more I thanked him. For I discovered that every broadside of condemnation hit a weak spot in my character or equipment, and by marking these vulnerable spots I could strengthen my battle-front. Any public service that I may now render has been largely due to the unconscious kindness of my enemies. How to arrive somewhere: Let your critic be your guide.

It is most encouraging to watch the trend of the world toward a universal application of the law of service. We find it everywhere — in commerce, finance, education, medicine, jurisprudence, reform, religion. Let us note a few recent examples.

HOW SERVICE SPREADS

The big automobile companies are establishing free "service stations" throughout the country for the benefit of customers; national manufacturers maintain "service departments" where counsel may be had without charge; some of the public utility corporations have reduced rates voluntarily, to meet the hard times and satisfy patrons; many of the great department stores provide special service to their visitors at less than cost; and the most famous merchant in the United States declares that he prefers the word "service" to the word "efficiency" as all efficiency is based on service.

The bankers have begun to formulate a system of rural credits and loans, thereby serving the huge agricultural populace; and to inculcate the habit of thrift by printing and circulating a set of instructions for personal means of saving. The teachers are giving free lectures to the parents of pupils; are visiting pupils in their homes; are turning the schoolhouse into a place of hospitality, a social service center. The doctors are abandoning drugs and substituting lessons in preventive hygiene; are distributing leaflets and bulletins, writing reports, books and magazine articles — all tending to deprive the doctor of his fee, but to serve his client more generously.

A commission has been appointed among lawyers, with ex-President Taft a member, to infuse more completely the spirit and fact of justice into the letter of the law; the office of "public defender" has been created for the righteous and impartial support of culprits who are without means; the night court, the juvenile court, and the woman probation officer all help to give a prisoner a square deal. Temperance reform takes on slowly the appearance not of hit-or-miss, holier-than-thou preaching, but of scientific, personal, sympathetic, detailed, study of the *causes* that lead to wrongdoing, and gentle, patient, psychological and biological treatment and removal of the cause. And in religion — the beautiful deeds of human service are the acknowledged proofs of strength in a church. Everywhere, the aim of progressive people now is to serve.

I have seen the president of a national institution cheerfully do the work of his office boy when the boy was suddenly called home to attend a sick mother. I have seen the world's richest young man put himself out to accommodate a fellow whose pocketbook and head were, to all appearances, equally empty. I have seen a dignitary who holds thirty offices — some of them international — go into the kitchen and wash dishes. Are you as proud to do the humblest work well as you would be to hold the highest position? Then you're of the stuff that big men are made of.

The principles and motives underlying efficient service are as broad as life itself. Here no technical barrier divides the teacher from the millhand, the corporation president from the lowest clerk in his employ. Your work may be in a store, a factory, an office, an attic, a theater, a bank, a home, a school, or a church; no matter, the ideas and ideals of genuine, satisfying service will appeal and apply to you as of direct personal use.

What are the first ten points in efficient service? We judge them to be as follows, and would commend them to you for analysis and comparison relating to your business or profession.

WHAT EFFICIENT SERVICE MEANS

1. *A keen sense of personal responsibility.* This seems largely lacking in the make-up of the American child, and is not fostered by our educational methods, which reward grades in school instead of growth in character. The founder of scientific management says that the greatest drawback to industrial advancement is the prevailing tendency of the American workman to "soldier" on the job; he has to be watched, warned and threatened, or he slumps into laziness and carelessness. The first sign of a good workman is that he does his best work unwatched. Moreover, a man's work pays him just what he feels he owes to his work, — little for little, much for much. The guarantee of our satisfaction and promotion is the willingness to sacrifice anything, everything, short of health and honor, to the claims of our calling.

2. *A scientific study of the needs and the wishes of our patrons.* The needs and the wishes do not always coincide, yet both should be granted. Thus, the largest newspaper in the United States prints flaming headlines, huge exposures, and volumes of political and "sporting" news — which is what people pay for; then provides the most thoughtful editorials and uplifting poems — which the people need, but wouldn't pay for. One of the biggest patent medicine concerns makes its remedy chiefly of colored water, then offers hygienic advice which does the work that the concoction is supposed to do. Many a public writer, now earning $5,000 to $12,000 a year, once declared himself unappreciated and the world all wrong simply because he had failed to study his market — he would submit farcical jibes to the Atlantic Monthly or philosophical dissertations to the Smart Set. Study the needs and wishes of your patrons.

3. *A fresh and full supply of the best goods.* This applies not only to merchandise, but to every commodity and service. The cry of today is always for something new, and the way to meet the demand is to supply what is both new and true.

KNOW YOUR GOODS

4. *A thorough knowledge of the goods and pride in the service.* Here is a much-neglected field. The price of a ribbon and its place on the shelf do not form the summation of knowledge for a clerk. The ribbon should match the complexion, taste, purse, temperament and design of the intending customer. How many ribbon clerks are trained to see all this at a glance? How many have learned the psychology of color? How many can tell where and how to secure any ribbon out of stock that the customer may wish? How many really enjoy being accommodating when the service costs a little trouble? "I haven't this "versus" We will get it

for you" — here in a clause we may note the difference between bad service and good service, and between bad salesmanship and good salesmanship.

5. *Technical training and superior skill.* To serve a patron effectively we must be able to do what he cannot, but must never show that we know we can. Here is where the average teacher falls short — he cannot teach in a superior fashion, but looks as though he could. He must learn from the scientific salesman. Probably 500,000 American business men have taken special courses in practical business training. I doubt if nearly as many teachers have so prepared themselves for their life work before engaging in it. Hence a great number have to face disappointment, sooner or later. Promotion without preparation is unethical and unscientific; but thousands of teachers look for it. Every ambitious man or woman, bent on achieving the most possible, should take a residence or correspondence course in the professional or industrial subject bearing directly on his vocational career.

6. *Psychological price and a fixed, frank policy.* The psychological price of a thing is what people think they can afford to pay. Thus a $1.50 article marked down to $1.49 satisfies cupidity and sells like hot cakes; while a $150 surgical operation marked up to $300 satisfies the awe and fear of the unknown, and is paid for without a murmur. To charge every cent that a commodity is worth, and not a cent more, is a fine test of commercial character. A new price plan, recently adopted by a national shoe company, a wealthy construction company, and a few other concerns, frankly and openly specifies "cost plus five per cent." (or ten per cent, as the case may be), and shows the customer an itemized bill of costs, proving the net gain to be as declared. This plan, taking your customer into your confidence, has points of merit worth noting.

7. *Cheerfulness without pay.* A little smiling service means more than a large frowning one. And smiles cost no energy, no money,

no pains, merely a bit of thoughtfulness and friendliness. A railroad company last year installed efficiency methods which tallied a reported saving of $6,000,000. One of the new features was the adoption of this slogan: "Our Patrons Are Our Guests" — and a corresponding mode of behavior. Hint for every business man: Be as cordial and obliging to everybody, stranger as well as customer, as though he were a guest in your home.

8. *Deference without servility.* And to the poor as well as to the rich. Here is a lovely Arabian Night's entertainment for a millionaire: Dress up in a beggar's old rags, then go shopping on Fifth Avenue; when each clerk or other menial snubs you, flash a $1000 bill on him or her, then deliver a lecture on the folly and sin of snubbing anybody, then report the offender to the management.

9. *Prompt and full adjustment of all complaints.* In every line of business, a method of reports, tabulations and results in the complaint and request department should be made to guarantee satisfaction to the patron. How do you make sure that every patron is always pleased? How will you make sure? One of the first rules for business prestige is to make every critic a friend.

10. *Your word is as good as your bond.* I would rather lose a finger than break my word in business. A lost finger means inconvenience, but a lost reputation means financial as well as moral suicide. And a promise to a clerk is more binding than a promise to the richest patron; the patron goes, but the clerk stays to scatter seeds of trouble. In trade, as in friendship, the supreme and winning force is fidelity. So the word "Truth" has been made the watchword of the world's largest club of advertising men. [Truth in promise, truth in performance, truth in ultimate purpose and immediate plan; here is the backbone of modern, broad, efficient service. To have your patron trust you as he would his best friend, this should be the aim and creed of every one who serves.

II. HEALTH

CHAPTER 7

A Sound Body and the Efficient Life

A MAN is a blend of animal and angel.

The proportions may vary — a prizefighter is mostly animal, a missionary mostly angel; but the animal and the angel are both in every man. The problem is, not to avoid either, but to improve the quality of each.

The trouble with us all is not that we are animals, but that we are poor animals. Every year we waste millions of dollars in the search for health, and also billions of foot-pounds of action-producing energy, because we have wandered from the paths of Nature and become enmired in the quicksands of a spurious intellectuality. Vitality is the mainstay of both mentality and spirituality.

Health should be taught systematically, thoroughly and attractively in every home, school and church of the world. And as men at large have lost their health-giving instincts, we should have to study the rules of hygiene from animals in the forest.

Is there any reason why we should build "model institutions" for the housing of the unfit, rather than learn how to prevent the occurrence of the unfit? As the world progresses, should new diseases (or at least new names for diseases) be multiplying with startling rapidity?

We have got this health matter wrong-end-to. We spent $100 in trying to regain health where we should spend $1 in learning to maintain health. We wake up only when we break down. Consequently we pay about $1,500,000,000 each year for this folly, which amount would be saved if we cared enough to prevent the unnecessary loss from disease and death in this country.

Probably the worst, certainly the most widespread, malady in America is *humanitis*, or a feverish desire to be supercivilized. The honest health in the shaggy, rough, crude elements of life has been replaced by a sickly assortment of hothouse refinements that avail for nothing but a social pride or indolence. The richer a man becomes, the less he does for himself; and for a man to be ill, some part of him must have been idle. We need to be saved from our servants and freed from our luxuries.

Consider the unhygienic day of the average "successful" man.

He has slept in a room overheated and underventilated. He rises late — and his whole day is immediately marked "Rush." He takes a perfunctory bath, neither hot enough to lubricate the bodily machine, nor cold enough to wake up the mind for the day.

His breakfast, swallowed hastily and unhungrily, chiefly consists of a creamed cereal with an acid fruit — a dietetic combination almost sure to start rebellion in the stomach.

He hurries for his street car, train or limousine, grabs a morning paper on the way, and while his vehicle jolts him downtown, he disturbs his vision, digestion and emotion by filling his mind with tragedies and trifles from all over the world, that have no bearing whatsoever on his usefulness for the day. Reaching the office with his stomach and brain both peevish and protesting, he starts the day's work in no fit condition for enduring the strain on eye, ear, brain and nerves that a modern day's work requires of a successful man. If he feels "out of sorts" he sends to the drug store for a headache powder — and commits further ruin of his stomach.

He works in foolish, inefficient clothes — from tight-fitting shoes to stiff, high collar. Never having learned the science of relaxation, he speeds on explosively, clear to the moment of going out for his one o'clock luncheon. He arrives at the restaurant deeply embedded in problems and cares, through which the gastric juices cannot percolate. More often than not, he talks up a "business deal" over coffee and cigars — a custom that, on scientific analysis, appears physiologically and psychologically unsound.

After his day of close confinement he hurries uptown, dresses in even more absurd clothes, eats a heavy dinner, then propels himself to an evening function that destroys the best sleeping hours — from ten to twelve — and finally drops into bed with a horrible sense of having to do the same thing over to-morrow, and to-morrow's tomorrow, and all the countless to-morrows of the rest of the days of his life.

What is wrong with this man? He simply does not know the meaning and purpose of civilization, he has made an end of the means to an end. The object of civilization is to develop the human brain, which it does to a nicety by the friction, competition, compulsion and routine of American life in the twentieth century. But while civilization strengthens our brain, civilization weakens our body. The endless train of chronic diseases was produced, and is perpetuated, by civilization. Only as a man uncivilizes, or decivilizes, himself during a certain portion of his time can he hope to attain great longevity coupled with great productivity.

We are now in the third stage of race unfoldment. In the babyhood of the race we were animals; in the childhood of the race we were beings of romance, adorers of myths, fables, dogmas, superstitions; in the manhood of the race we are mental or industrial machines; in the supermanhood of the race we shall be liberated spirits, having brains, hearts and bodies fully developed, but using and commanding them as conscious owners of them. The third, or mind stage, is the least healthy of them all; since it lacks the enduring strength of the body stage, the vitalizing faith of the heart stage, or the renewing poise of the soul stage.

Let us now regard the superior wisdom of animals, in habits, customs and instincts pertaining to health. Nature is the true guide to health; and in the multiplicity of modern cures, cults, pathies, ologies and isms, our safety lies in recourse to Nature. While medicine, psychology and surgery may be needed in acute cases of specific diseases, a purely natural mode of living is the best health preservative. We can learn this from the animals, in the following respects:

1. *Natural food.* — The animals eat only when hungry, of the simplest articles, for the sole purpose of satisfying hunger. Myriads of human beings eat three meals a day — and are never hungry. To be hungry, you must feel your mouth water at the very thought of a slice of plain whole wheat bread and butter. If, as we are told, ninetenths of all our ailments proceed from bad digestion, we may well say that disease was born halfway between the cook stove and the menu card. For most of the foods that need to be cooked need more to be corrected, and the deadliness of dinners lies in their variety. Who of us would make a slab of raw meat the piece de resistance at a banquet? Hosts of common disorders may be ascribed largely to the modern vogue of mixing all kinds of food stuffs, first in the cook stove, then on the menu card.

An ideal lunch, containing the elements to support life and satisfy hunger, is a piece of graham bread and butter, a poached egg, a glass of pure milk, and a baked apple. How many people, entertaining at luncheon, would dare to order a meal like that? Six leading dishes are enough for any meal. Yet some of our noblest statesmen, being feted and banqueted, have to go to bed with an old-fashioned stomach ache due to the "hospitality" of their popularity. Real hospitality means filling the hearts, minds and souls of our friends — not their stomachs. And I look forward to the time when the only eatable offered to a passing guest will be a delicious, refreshing beverage — hot in winter, cold in summer, and more respectful of his digestion than of our pride.

2. *Natural sleep.* — The animals sleep while the world is dark, wake when their sleep is out, and perfectly relax during the process. We men and women turn night into day and lose three or four hours at the beginning of our night's rest; consequently we depend on the alarm clock to rouse us when we should be sleeping, and we sleep under a usual nervous tension, brought on by home or business cares, midnight pleasures, or beds and bedclothes and bedrooms that have no bearing at all on the matter of sleep. For most people in American civilization, the healthful hours of sleep are from ten P. M. to six or seven A. M. Once or twice a week it is permissible, and I think psychologically desirable, to postpone bedtime an hour or so; and occasionally, to vary the monotony of things, one may even stay up all night. But a fixed and wholesome retiring hour is one of the imperative needs of our life. Incomplete and insufficient sleep is a large factor in the host of nervous troubles now afflicting Americans.

The bed is the most important piece of furniture in the house. One of the bad habits of American life is the prevalence of the narrow single bed, which violates the principle of the necessity of motion obtaining even in rest. No man can sleep right on a couch three feet wide. Unconsciously, we change our posture during sleep — it is no more natural to hold the same position during eight hours of slumber than during eight hours of waking consciousness. The bed should be wide enough and long enough to allow full stretching, in comfort, on all sides. A thick, sanitary mattress, warranted to stay smooth; a set of unbreakable springs, affording the utmost buoyance; an outfit of coverlets extra long to tuck in well at the bottom; a thin pillow, and a porous night garment everywhere loose, particularly around the neck; — these are a few essentials of natural sleep. The great principle is to keep the feet warm and head cool, as the depth of slumber is proportional to the departure of blood from the head. The pillow should be less than six inches through, and as hard as may be comfortable. Soft, thick pillows are made for soft, thick heads.

3. *Natural exercise.* — The animals are forced to exercise, in order to obtain food; but their play consists of exercise, which is to them not irksome but enjoyable. The opposite holds among men. The higher a man gets, the more he sits. Nothing can ever take the place of outdoor physical exercise, which is the automatic regulator of digestion, respiration, circulation, elimination. Every brainworker, to keep "fit" mentally as well as physically, should have an hour in the open every day, occupying himself with a brisk walk, a horse-back ride, an athletic game, or some other physiological tonic in the form of muscular movement.

4. *Natural baths.* — The animals are given a constant process of hardening and health — ensured by having their bodies exposed to the weather. Likewise, the human body was made to be rained upon — see how quickly the small boy hastens out, umbrella-less and unbeknownst, into the midst of a summer shower. A primary sign of health is that you enjoy a bath, whatever the season of the year. But a cold bath should never meet a cold body; and, unless one has a great store of reserve energy, the morning ablution should be tempered sufficiently to avoid shock. It is said that water may be used in a thousand different ways, for the preservation or recovery of health. Every man, woman and child should know on principle and by experience the kind and

number and variation of the baths, weekly or daily, best suited to the temperament, nature and need of the individual.

5. *Natural air.* The animals continually bathe their lungs in oxygen, they do not fear "drafts," they let the refreshing, invigorating breezes play on their bodies day and night, summer and winter, the whole year through. But in our cities, where human animals are supposed to be most efficient, there are thousands of shops, factories, tenements and flats whose inhabitants never get pure air till hot weather makes them open the windows. Airing a house once a day is not enough — every window should be kept always open, if only an inch at the top. There are patent ventilators which deflect the cold currents of outside air and gradually diffuse the oxygen through the room. A most healthful habit is to take an air-bath just before going to bed, wearing simply bathrobe and sandals and moving briskly about for ten or fifteen minutes, all windows being wide open. We do not fear exposure to the elements, we fear exposure of our fear of the elements. Anybody who has outgrown the fear of pure air sufficiently to try a sleeping porch for a few months will tell you how impossible it is for a really healthy person to sleep in the four great walls and one little window that we call a bedroom.

6. *Sunshine.* The animals are vitalized, disinfected and asepticized by sunshine, which is the greatest germicide, cleanser and tonic known to science. If a way could be invented to bottle sunlight, and sell it to sick folks at an exorbitant price, the inventor would be a billionaire in no time at all. We need more windows in our houses, for not one house in fifty has enough. A house should be regarded merely as a frame for sunlight. Every man who builds a home should plan a sun parlor for it; a sun parlor is much more hygienic than a society parlor. I would not, in fact, recommend that much light be admitted to an ordinary parlor; this, being a stuckup kind of room, would melt if the sun fell on it. In every disease there is a broad streak of artificiality.

Let us flood our homes and hearts with light; let us tear away the heavy curtains from our windows and our minds; let us realize that health is only truth made over into life. And to have truth direct we must seek God and Nature. God is healer of the soul, Nature is healer of the body; when we have learned and applied this fact, we shall mightily increase the length and the strength of our lives. For the way to be well is not to swallow something, but to learn something — then live it!

CHAPTER 8

Unused Powers[*]

"**Y**OU are a potential giant.

"But you are an actual dwarf.

"How can you help being restless, irritable, unhappy — while a buried volcano, of energy lies in the depths of your nature?"

This was the diagnosis recently given a friend of the writer by a skilled physician of the soul. The truth of it is almost universal. Magnificent possibilities lie unexplored, undiscovered, unimagined, within the mental recesses and spiritual treasure-troves common to us all. Only a crisis — a great responsibility, a matchless opportunity, a sudden death or disaster — avails to rouse and develop these unused powers. Lacking the crisis, we are prone to sleep or fritter our lives away.

The transcendental problem of humanity is to be as great always as one can be at rare moments. Men are as great as they force themselves to use themselves. Genius is but an irresistible urge to be occupied. The man who succeeds has become a self-winding watch on his own

---

* Please note: this essay was originally published as a portion of chapter 1 of Efficient Living (1915)

movements, so that he knows by intuition when he is either running down or wearing himself out. (Starvation is the best remedy for underaction, sleep the best remedy for over-action.)

There is no error unattended by repression. We make mistakes because we are deficient in the power to see, or in the power to do as we see. But spiritual sight and sinew may be cultivated, will be cultivated systematically in the ages to come. The time is fast approaching when only a *spiritual* Hercules can move the world. Mental giants rule now, but their crude force merely corresponds to the primitive condition of the race. First body-rule, now brain-rule, next heart-rule, finally soul-rule; this is the plan of worldsovereignty.

What are some of the unused powers that we own but do not turn to advantage?

Unused *muscles*, unused *lungs*, unused *instincts*, unused *emotions*, unused *perceptions*, unused *faculties*, unused *ideals*.

Unused muscles cripple us. Not externally, but vitally. If you ever witnessed the marvelous feats performed by Sandow or any other "strong man," you know what a beautiful network of muscles envelop and support the fine torso of the trained athlete — his body is a work of art. But do you know that his superb digestion is maintained largely by these interlaced muscular fibers, which hold the digestive organs in true position, thus enabling them to act freely? Are you anaemic, thin, troubled with poor circulation? Then look to the muscles of arms and legs; for live blood follows live muscle, and where there is weak assimilation there is weak sinew. So apparently remote a thing as sleep is affected by muscular condition; if your sleep is fitful, and your body tied in a bow-knot, your back muscles and shoulder muscles need attention — their flabbiness permits the spine to crook and the chest to sag, hence the nerves cannot relax nor the blood circulate. Withered muscles work havoc throughout the whole system.

Unused lungs cripple us. The majority of civilized people exert only a fraction of their normal breathing capacity; and a host of ills, from brain-fag and ennui to dyspepsia and hysteria, come from this defect in respiration. Great singers, champion swimmers, and other such lungdevelopers, are usually marvels of robustness. On taking sudden exercise, do you feel dizziness, vertigo, or rush of blood to the head? Then your lung chambers have been short of oxygen, since the effort to fill them causes unaccustomed pressure, which you feel accordingly. How long can you hold your breath without discomfort? If for a minute or longer, you may be glad of a pair of lungs that know their business and stick to it. The lungs are the organs of liberation; exercised deeply and regularly, they free us mentally and spiritually as well as physically. Conquerors have often been men of small stature — but of gigantic breathing power. From Cromwell on the battlefield to Beecher in the pulpit, the takers of the world's citadels have found their source of power in the breath.

Unused instincts cripple us. The instinct of the animal guards him against foes, against poisons, against all outer perils known or unknown. At the approach of danger, the snail retreats in his shell, the porcupine bristles, the deer flees with the wind. Yet we, who are supposed to know more, do less. We regularly eat what we know isn't good for us, allowing poison, in quality or quantity, to enter the system through the mouth; we are guided by appetite instead of by hunger; we choke our food down when we should rest and ruminate; we add tonics and peptonizers to the gastronomic insult — then we sadly complain how afflicted we are with a poor stomach! Moreover, we entertain as regular guests such thoughts as lead to mental paralysis and spiritual decrepitude — worry, fear, jealousy, doubt, dependence, deceit, compromise. The snail, the deer and the porcupine would do it better. In the presence of such intruders we must cultivate our shell, our sinews of flight, or our bristles if need be.

Unused emotions cripple us. The height of our attainment is directly proportioned to the depth of our feeling. All great men have one trait in common; a fierce intensity, which annihilates all things superficial and irrelevant. Convention forbids this — convention thrives on pettiness. It is not "good form" to feel deeply; it is good form to die prematurely, the coffin is the symbol of good form. So long as the favorite disease of fashion is repression, so long will nerves be the favorite symptoms of fashion. We might almost say that no man is healthy who has not experienced a sublime joy or an overwhelming sorrow. Our emotions extend us into a realm divine, the knowledge of which provides our human lives with infinite capacity for growth. To feel deeply is to understand the world; to feel nobly is to penetrate the heavens; to feel strongly is to force Fate.

Unused perceptions cripple us. Until we escape the dominion of the senses, we dwell in chaos personified. That is why the Oriental mystic refuses to converse, to eat, to shake hands, to see his friends, to enjoy music or perfume, until his outer senses have been silenced, that his inner sensibilities may be uttered. The selfbanishment of Tolstoi on the eve of death, after his self-deprivation through life, was but an echo of the world-old cry of the soul to be loosed from the flesh, and perceive more clearly with the trammels gone. We cannot all be sages, seers or mystics, we have work to do on the earth-plane; but we can all recognize the presence of finer forces about us, and so attune ourselves as to hear and voice in our own way the heavenly strains of the Great Monition. You tell me that prayer exalts the soul. I tell you that prayer clears the eye, steadies the hand, calms the nerve, quickens the judgment, strengthens the will, makes the whole man keen, alert, and sure. The non-religious man is a dwarf in his subjective nature. He is to be pitied, not condemned.

Unused faculties cripple us. What can we do best? Are we doing it? Can we find in our work full scope and play for our talents? Are we consciously progressing every day toward a fixed goal? These questions are of life-long and earthwide importance. Every human being is a conglomeration of plus and minus qualities, which must be classified, arranged, unified, before the personal equation is solved. There should be in every college a department of Character Study, devoted to the recognition, measurement and equalization of the strong and weak faculties of the youth who attend. The human brain has some forty odd powers, traits and talents struggling for expression. Prominent are these: Individuality, Continuity, Courage, Combativeness, Self-esteem, Sociability, System, Language, Music, Poetry, Invention, Parenthood, Ideality, Hope. The warrior is weak in Ideality, the poet weak in Continuity, the pedagogue weak in Combativeness, the hermit weak in Sociability, the cynic weak in Hope. Yet each is strong in his own peculiar field. The problem of life is so to choose our field that our strength may be apparent.

Unused ideals cripple us. An ideal is a premonition of power. The idealist often squanders or fails to use his power — then the onlooker blames the ideal. There is nothing so dangerous to the spiritual life as to conceive an ideal, undertake a pilgrimage for it, then turn back. It is like entering a path over a chasm so narrow and steep that one false step means destruction, and you have not time to pause, or room to retreat. These are the marching orders given the idealist: "On and up — or die!" Remain blind if you will, to your own possibilities on earth, and the glories of the heavens beyond. But having sought your vision, and beheld one thing clearly, follow that to the end. Nothing worse than death awaits. And to fall amid the peaks, with the sun full upon you, is a death that angels might envy.

"How then may we find and free ourselves?"

Perhaps you are asking this — every honest thinker must ask it sooner or later.

There is no easy way, no quick way, no cheap way. The effective way is hard, and long, and painful. But all the great souls who ever lived have trod this way. And the greater the soul, the greater the willingness.

Always choose the hardest thing.

But the hardest thing grows easy when you like to do it. Learn your facility, and smoothe the rough corners of destiny.

Associate with people who have developed themselves, who *do* things — not merely have things. The social climber is right in method, if not in motive; the way to get ahead is to follow those who have arrived. Do you enjoy being with those whom you know are superior to yourself? Then your powers are in line for development.

But call no man your superior, call the man ahead merely your predecessor; call yourself as great as the greatest, then live up to the acclamation.

Be much alone. Solitude is the birthplace of strong ideas, fine plans and healthy purposes.

Ask some kind friend to tell you exactly what he thinks of you. Double his praise, and his censure. Then you will get a fair idea both of what you may become, and of what you now are. No friend ever saw our best — or dared paint our worst.

Keep in touch with the current literature of your business or profession. If you are a merchant or a metaphysician, a doctor or a manufacturer, a housewife or a teacher, there are books and magazines being published that would greatly expedite your work, by suggesting ways to economize your expenditure of time, thought and money. Whatever vocation you pursue, keep in touch with the best minds and let your brain be constantly sharpened with new ideas from any source available.

Learn to save motions in your work. This will give you time for something more valuable than work.

Acquire mastery of one thing at a time. It is a joy to master words, a joy to master thoughts, a joy to master acts, a joy to master feelings, a joy to master events, a joy to master people. But each of these forms of mastery is a study in itself; whoever is a graduate in one branch of mastery should forthwith enter another.

Make a thorough, systematic, persistent, study of the opportunities around you. Discontented people are merely blind. There are gates opening all the time, which the majority do not see because they are looking either at the stars or in the mud. A willingness to face life clears away most of the shadows that merely touch life.

Have faith in your dream. It is the seed of your destiny, let no gust of Fate sweep it away, no man despoil you of it, no battle crush it. Out of dreams grow empires. We are masters of Fate and owners of the world, while still we have our dream in our grasp.

CHAPTER 9

Save Your Nerves

THE great American folly is hurry. We do everything in a hurry. We work, play, eat, sleep, talk, walk, think, read, write, pray, love and marry — all in a hurry. We are the greatest hurriers — and the greatest worriers — on the globe.

The end of hurry is worry; since hurry makes blunders and blunders breed confusion. Whether we know it or not, half of worry is hurry. When a man does his best and takes his time doing it, he instinctively trusts God to crown his work with happiness.

As a nation, we are tense without being intense — a psychological waste and physiological menace. The great worrier is tense without being intense — the great worker intense without being tense. A common trait of the captains of industry and the leaders of science is their nerve poise; whether it be Rodin carving a statue, or Burbank evolving a plant, or Edison molding an invention, or Morgan building a railroad, or Kitchener calling five million men to the colors — the mark of the man is calm, a supreme certainty born of a supreme skill. He who frets fears failure.

More and more do our nerves become the channels of our destiny. Through them pours the energy, by them grows the courage, in them lies the health to achieve great things. Of all the portions and functions of the body, the nerves are the most difficult to repair. And the greatest waste in American life is waste of nerve force.

HOW WE WASTE NERVE FORCE

We eat too much, too fast and too often. We talk with the reserve, sweetness and composure of a boiler factory. We live and work amid countless and needless noises. We measure our neighbor by his speed-record and his bank-book. We put the clock where the altar used to be. We entertain too frequently, gaudily and politely. We read bales of trash, and wonder why our thought scatters and our memory fades out. We tie ourselves to a schedule as we tie a dog to his post, then we cannot see why we lack initiative, courage, magnetism. We dress to enrich the fashion-mongers, not to ennoble ourselves. We roam where the bright lights dazzle, but never look at the darkness ahead. We buy more and more tonics, and habit-forming drugs. Millions of us go to the moving pictures every day — and a three-hour focus of the mind on the film play and vaudeville wastes enough energy to start a man well toward a better job. We batter our nerves this way and that for no reason except that we follow the crowd, and refuse to listen to ourselves.

I know of many a speed-maniac and efficiency fanatic who rather takes pride in the fact that he keeps going all the time. So does an empty hogshead, going down hill. The quickest way to run down is to be always speeding up. When you watch your watch and not yourself, watch out!

A regular duty of an efficient man is to forget to be efficient. The time to observe this duty is every Sunday, two or three evenings a week, and three or four weeks a year. Otherwise efficiency becomes an obsession; and the more moral an obsession is, the more dangerous it is. Very earnest souls often ask me if the loss of time does not worry me fearfully? I tell them "Surely — I don't lose enough!" No system is complete without a system to forget system. First lesson in achievement — how to work; second lesson — how to stop working. The productive mind is creative; and essential to the finest creations are the long relaxations between.

Fifty years ago about two-thirds of the people of the United States lived in the country. Now, only about one-third live there; the rest have moved business or home, or both, to the city centers of noise, congestion, irritation, competition and worry. No such rapid and complete change of national environment was ever known before in the history of the nations of the world.

We have not become properly adjusted to the new conditions. Our grandfathers needed health of muscle — and they got it on the farm. We need health of nerve — and we get it nowhere. The subject is not taught or even understood, by parents or physicians or college professors. We are never trained in the function, use and care of the nerves until the nerves break down and we are laid on the shelf. Moreover, it is the people of fine talents and great possibilities who are subject to nerve disorders; human kine don't get nervous prostration — human lions do. This fact makes nerve protection a vital study and urgent need in the conservation of our best national resources — the men and women who might do great things.

Now relaxation is the key to the nerve problem. The final efficiency test of a great worker is that he knows how to rest. This knowledge, rightly used, will add five or ten years to his life, will save him future sanitarium bills and loss of time when most needed, will augment the quality and quantity of his yearly brain output by fifteen to thirty per cent, and will help him to be an example of sane living to all his friends.

By "relaxation" I do not mean play, diversion or amusement. Play is merely change of motion. Relaxation is cessation of motion, and solitude. Make your mind a perfect blank, let your nerves and muscles hang as limp as though you had lost control of them, blur all consciousness of time, care and responsibility, close your eyes and ears to all sensation, feel nothing, want nothing, remember nothing, hold nothing, revel softly in a dreamy haze of oblivion while the hours slip away unmarked and unmeasured, be as calm and inert as a moss-grown log in a shady dell where the soothing willows gently wave and flowers breathe content beside a sleepy brook.

POWER THROUGH RELAXATION

The power to relax is the *source* of the power to concentrate. The human soul is like a mountain reservoir. Quietly and slowly, away from the multitude, it fills and renews itself with strength, purpose, faith, courage, energy, speed, initiative. Then it pours down through the world and moves the mills of trade like a Niagara! But first, in relaxation, the power must accumulate. A man can no more be efficient without a proper mode of relaxation than a system of electric light or motion could be without a fully charged battery. When we are dull, tired, cross, perplexed, discouraged, we should simply remember the nerves are electric wires, needing a new life. We must learn to relax, for the sake of our health, work, prosperity, influence, growth.

Our health demands relaxation. In the United States child mortality is decreasing, but middleage mortality increasing — we have more cases, annually, of heart disease, apoplexy, nervous prostration, exhaustion, presenility and insanity. Cause? Too rapid living, candle burnt at both ends, light goes out. Cure? Knowledge and habit of relaxation, in early life. The only sure cure is prevention.

Our work demands relaxation. The great work is done by the genius, who forgets to eat and sleep while he hammers his dream into shape, melted with divine fire and molded at the forge of concentration. But his work done, the genius grows lax, idle, care-free as a child. The ebb and flow of spirit, like the ebb and flow of the sea, must be regarded. While we are machines we are bound to routine; but as we learn to create, we must counterbalance creation with relaxation. I know a man who, after a long stress of powerful creative work, slept an average of fourteen hours a day for a month. Then he was ready for a new feat of empire building. To be alert be inert before and after. To do more, do nothing between times.

Our prosperity demands relaxation. The money-making ideas come to the man who is mentally and physically fresh and vigorous. Capacity measures opportunity, and our chance is as great as our power to seize it with all the grip of our magnetic forces. A friend of mine, starting on nothing, has built up a huge business, from which he has taken several fortunes. His secret, you ask? He answers "Money is productivity, productivity is energy and I have learned how to *renew by energy*, pouring a flood of it into my business whenever the finances threaten to be low."

Our influence demands relaxation. Our neighbors like us, listen to us, follow us, when we are strong, keen, sure, bright and sunny. A fag in a man is a drag on all his friends. To restore cheeriness, cure fatigue. And to be a leader of men, be a follower of Nature; draw from earth and air and water, sun and sky, the magnetic forces to rejuvenate you, and others through you.

Our growth demands relaxation. We are citizens of Cosmos, dwellers in Eternity, heirs of Infinity. Why then hurry? Why fret and grieve at delay or disappointment? Everything must come right when *we* are right. We cannot sow a panic and reap a destiny. Moral vision, even more than physical vitality, must be conserved and refreshed by wholesome, normal periods of seclusion, meditation, relaxation, reunion with God and Nature.

We are industrial pragmatists. Our answer is to every business theory: "Does it *work?*" Has the regular observance of the need to relax produced results to justify our claim? It has. We cite cases.

One of the world's richest men finds that his afternoon work is greatly improved by a siesta following lunch. A famous captain of industry keeps a lounge in his office, and when the cares and duties of his strenuous life press too close, he resorts to silence, locks the doors, muffles the telephone, draws the blinds, forgets business, lies limp and relaxed for ten or fifteen minutes — and speeds back to his desk, a new man! Certain large factories have reduced their working hours from ten to nine, or nine and a half, or even eight hours, without diminishing their output — the workers move faster when less tired, and feel better, mentally and physically. New York department stores have tried the experiment of closing all day Saturday in summer, to give their employees more chance to relax; and they have noted an actual increase of business in some cases, by having one business day less in the week. So slight a rest period as a fifteen minute recess in the middle of the afternoon for mill and factory workers has materially reduced the number of errors and accidents, most of which, due to fatigue, have been found to occur late in the afternoon. It pays financially to learn to relax.

The interested reader may ask when, where and how? We offer brief suggestions, particularly for the hard-working, fast-thinking man or woman who is highly organized, ambitious and intense.

Be on your guard against the hurry habit. Systematize your day and plan your work ahead, so you never need to hurry. When you have appointments to keep, always give yourself a leeway of five or ten minutes to provide for unexpected hindrances and prevent last-moment rushes. Move slowly, speak slowly, think and feel slowly, outside of office hours. Finish every piece of work before you start another. Change the stress and strain of your daily routine from your nerves to your muscles — you can do it by the proper system of mental and physical exercise. Learn to like slow, phlegmatic people, and be much in their company; you will irritate them as much as they do you, and the combined friction should wear away some of the eccentricities of you both. Cultivate the friendship of day-laborers, and spend an evening often with them; people who work their brains only are about as restful, for constant companions, as a roomful of clocks in perfect health.

Study books on nerve-control. Read regularly one hygienic and one psychological magazine; but not more, please, than one each, lest you become a hopeless health crank and sicker than would otherwise be possible. Choose for your doctor one who is a trained psychologist — as every doctor should be — the physical troubles of a keen brain-worker are likely to be mostly nervous in origin, therefore, amenable to psychic treatment only.

Wear soft, loose clothing — no stiff hats or corsets. No high collars, no tight shoes, no wool next the skin. Get the Blucher form of shoe, preferably of vici kid, and have rubber heels on every pair. At home use moccasins or sandals, or a patent cushion slipper, even more restful than these, and obtainable at almost any shoe store. Let all your colors of your dress and your room be quiet, peaceful, harmonizing with your taste and temperament. Choose plain, simple furniture of the mission or similar type; avoid rocking chairs, but have a reclining steamer or camp chair in your room, to conform to the body and give the perfect relaxation that a hammock does.

Have your only room lamp a powerful desk portable, fully shaded. Find a spot in your room where all the window light will strike your back and none your face. Then put your writing desk or reading table there. Get a miniature clock that ticks almost without being heard, or hang your watch on the wall; a loud ticking timepiece is hard on the nerves. Let your pictures be few and far between and your trinkets and ornaments even less. The proverbial calm of the nun is due partly to the wide spaces in her cloistered cell, and her vision is thus kept clear and tranquil.

RELAX RESOLUTELY

Be alone some time each day, and suffer motion to yield to meditation. Learn to speak seldom and slowly. When you read books omit the sensational novel of the present day and relax with Emerson, Carlyle, Whitman, Thoreau, Confucius, Epictetus, Marcus Aurelius. And prefer old-fashioned music to the ragtime of the modern cabaret. The chant of the cathedral organ is a clear invitation to repose. Take long walks when time is abundant. Make friends with night; commune with the stars, let them soothe away your cares.

Develop your will and dominate your wishes. Think great thoughts, and sweep away trifles. Plan a daily schedule with the right baths, foods and exercises to keep your nerves ready, steady, strong. Leave the "nerve tonic" sold in a bottle strictly alone, as it merely tones up the pocketnerve of the maker. Test the regenerating power of slow, calm, deep rhythmic breathing as a lifehabit. Experience the wonderful results on the nervous system of the air, light, sun and earth baths, now so popular in Europe.

Investigate the action of heat on the nerves, whether in a hot water bottle at spine or feet, a vapor bath, a prolonged submergence in very hot water, a cabinet for electric-light baths, or a hand thermal device for local use. (But first consult your physician.) When the nerves grow tense from overwork or anxiety have an expert apply massage to the head, spine and nerve branches.

Sleep sixty hours a week or more, and as nearly out doors as possible. Have your bed, springs, mattress, coverlets hygienic and scientific — here economy is out of place. Be asleep at ten o'clock half the nights in the week. Don't be ashamed to rest in the daytime — many a business man, otherwise sane, has gone to pieces and his business with him because when tired and worried he failed to rest by day — he thought he might look foolish, womanish or sickish if he lay down before dark! Always rest a few moments before and after meals. Relax on the street-car, going to and from business. Lock your work in the office and play with the children, or putter in the garden, or even lead the dog out for an airing, to clear your brain of business cobwebs in advance of dinner. Learn to change your consciousness as you change your coat, and make your home self utterly different from your business self.

A man's work lives to the extent that he lives for his work. To live for your work you must first live wholly in it — then wholly away from it. The force in concentration is the rebound from relaxation.

More work is good, better work is better, greater work is best. The man who does great work is so much greater than his work that he looks on all work as child's play; so he can smile at himself for working, when he is not working, and relax, and let go, and cease to think and do, in order just to *be*. The crown of achievement is attainment; and the measure of attainment is silent self-command.

EFFICIENCY NERVE TEST

FOR INDICATING PROBABLE CONDITIONS OF STRESS AND STRAIN OF THE
KEEN BRAIN WORKER, AND SUGGESTING RELAXATION METHODS FOR
HEALTH, POISE AND PRODUCTIVITY

DIRECTIONS. Read first the accompanying article by Mr. Purinton for a general view of the subject. Where answer to the question is Yes, write numeral 5 in black space opposite. Where answer is No, leave space blank. Add column for your approximate percentage in efficient nerve action. If your percentage is below 80, you need to study and practise the art of relaxation.

1. Can you relax perfectly as described in the article herewith? _____

2. Are you entirely free from hurry, worry, headache, nervousness, mental depression? _____

3. Do you know how to relieve pain, exhaustion or depletion of the nerves? _____

4. Is your doctor a nerve specialist? _____

5. Are you informed on the foods, baths and exercises to build and renew the nerves? _____

6. Have you made a study of personal conservation of energy? _____

7. Do you forget business on Sunday, and most of the evenings of the week? _____

8. Can you smile in the face of panic, epidemic, failure, grief and disappointment? _____

9. Is your daily schedule planned so as to
   avoid haste, waste, fatigue? _____

10. Do you rest fifteen to thirty minutes after
    each meal? _____

11. Are you a sound sleeper, and in bed sixty
    hours a week? _____

12. Are you thoroughly rested when you get
    up in the morning? _____

13. Would you rather be alone than "in
    society"? _____

14. Are your best friends the great philosophers
    of the past and present? _____

15. Have you studied a book on nerve control,
    and do you take a psychological journal? _____

16. Is cathedral music more pleasing to you
    than dance music? _____

17. Do you feel younger every year, and look
    much younger than you are? _____

18. Are you two different people — one at
    home and another at work? _____

19. Is the future a treasure-house of hopes,
    dreams, plans and purposes? _____

20. Do people, when in trouble, come to you
    for help and advice? _____

_____

Total equals your approximate grade in efficiency of nerve control.

III. HAPPINESS

CHAPTER 10

How to Achieve Happiness

IN our heart of hearts, we all crave Happiness.

This is the universal hunger. And only as we are satisfied do we feel that life is good.

Consciously or unconsciously, we have made Happiness the object of all our endeavor. We plan, toil, strive, save, suffer, hope and pray for it; we count no price too great, no sacrifice too costly — if only we may be sure of it. With it we ask for nothing else — without it we find the whole world empty and meaningless.

Even those who do not want to be happy are happiest when most unhappy. So that, like the rest of us, they too have joined the everlasting pilgrimage.

Consider for a moment how deep the longing is, and how fundamental to human activity.

The little child, before he can fairly lisp, stretches out his wee hands for a toy that some one has given him. Why? Because he thinks *play will make him happy*. And it will — for a time.

The lad of ambition sacrifices everything to his books or his athletic sports, holding even food secondary. He thinks *conquest will make him happy*. And it will for a time.

The lassie of romance bedecks herself in finery and waits all breathless for the coming of her Prince. She thinks a lover's *adoration will make her happy*. And it will for a time.

The owner of a business toils and plans and worries fifteen hours a day, while his employees begrudge eight. He thinks *work will make him happy*. And it will for a time.

The employee looks first, last and always for quick promotion with larger pay. He thinks *independence will make him happy*. And it will for a time.

The poet starves in his garret, asking nothing but to be left alone with his dream. He thinks *inspiration will make him happy*. And it will for a time.

The bride severs instantly the bonds of a lifetime, plunging bravely into a vast unknown future. She thinks *motherhood will make her happy*. And it will for a time.

The old, old man sits musing by the hearth as the evening shadows fall, searching the embers for something that can never be again. He thinks *memory will make him happy*. Perhaps it will, for a time.

Happiness, just Happiness, is what we all are seeking. Some are finding — and losing again. Some are almost touching — and feeling it slip from their grasp. A few are making their own, which they keep — if they are willing to share it. Whilst the many — blind, selfish, frantic — are cursing an imaginary fate that is only the projection of their own blurred thought. Weary of the struggle, some have declared Happiness a will-o'the-wisp, impossible to capture and resting in delusion. But this is only because they themselves do not see. They have chosen the wrong road, or wandered into a by-path, or fallen by the way — and paid for the error with bruises. Not because they follow a vision, but because they rush headlong, do the seekers of Happiness come to grief. Happiness dwells just over the horizon. And until we lift our eyes we cannot know the path.

What does all this mean?

Is Happiness right, as the first object of endeavor? If not, why do we want it? If so, why do we fail to get it?

The answer is this: *Really wanting a thing makes it right to have but hard to get.* The answer needs explaining. Nobody really wants Happiness — what everybody wants is Growth. But the majority, seeing only the fruit of development, which is Happiness, fail to consider the long hard months of pushing up through the earthen crust that lies between the seed and the fruitage. So, during growing-time, we are apt to feel impatient.

When a little toddler is just learning to walk, the father does not prepare a scientific treatise on the benefits of exercise to a juvenile organism. Father says with a cheery tone and a winning smile, "Baby, see that big red apple across the room? You may have it if you reach it before it's gone!" And Baby, forgetting he cannot walk, just walks.

We are the babies, the morsel of fruit is Happiness, and the All-wise Father keeps the reward before us while we are learning, through bruises and tears, to walk alone. Thus to be always reaching for Happiness is to be a child in God's nursery. When we are grown, we see that we have only been learning how to walk.

What is Happiness? This question has never been fully answered except by the one who asked it.

For Happiness is as many different things as there are different people. Each must find his own, or go without. And here is where most of the confusion arises. We presume to borrow Happiness from our neighbors, inherit it from our ancestors, beg it from our friends, or steal it from our enemies; then if only misery comes we blame Fate instead of our obtuseness.

The Happiness of Napoleon would have been torture to Shelley — and the Happiness of Shelley would have been irritation to Napoleon. Shelley was a fluttering, poignant, winged thing, whose joy was to soar with the skylark that he sang of; Napoleon was a great rigid monster of destruction, moved by the blast of the north wind and exulting in a world lying wrecked. The warrior took his Happiness from Nature — the poet took his from God. Ages of human experience, infinities of human longing, lay between.

Accordingly; to know what will make us happy, we must know where we are in the scale of evolution. Are we mostly animal — or mostly angel? Of the first, we need not be ashamed; of the last, we neet not be afraid. Human life at best is nothing more than a temporary bridge to lead us from the rugged bounds of Nature into the fragrant realms of God. To want to be human for the sake of being human is to have for one's highest ambition the lonesome little sentry-box of a watchman on a bridge. We are not fully human until the heart and body of us hunger most for the *natural wisdom* of bird and flower and jungle-beast; while the mind and soul of us thirst as much for the *heavenly understanding* of angel, star, and seraph. Being happy is just being whole.

There are women who, like the dove, are happy only when expressing tenderness; there are men who, like the lion, are happy only when expressing strength. And there are, now and then, full-grown humans having in them some of the dove, some of the lion, some of a thousand other primal ancestors unknown or long-forgotten. To these latter, Happiness is a complex and painful object of endeavor. We all know people who are in anguish to-day, in ecstasy to-morrow. We think them "queer" — because we cannot understand them. They are great souls unable for the time to use themselves. The person called an "enigma" is some one all finished but the handle; while they who call him that are only just begun. A good way to be happy is to look back a million years to the worm we have been, then look on, a million ages, to the god we shall become; then smile at the foolish vexations and meaningless tragedies filling a life that takes but a moment.

Verify this doctrine of human evolution.

The next time you ride in a street car, examine the faces lined up for easy inspection. You will discover a variety of animals masquerading as men — and perhaps a variety of angels in embryo. There may be donkeys, rats, foxes, parrots, and turkey gobblers. Or there may be tigers, elephants, greyhounds, eagles, and birds of Paradise. Can you imagine a rhinoceros telling a fawn how to be happy? It may be just as difficult for me to tell you, or for you to tell me. What we can do is tell each other how to tell ourselves. And that is the purpose of this book.

This brings us to our conclusion regarding Happiness, as follows:

Human beings are the only earth-inhabitants that are proverbially, chronically, and consistently unhappy. Animals are themselves — men and women are not. And that explains. Our food, our clothing, our dwellings, our books, our amusements, our habits and restrictions of work, even our education and theology, are mostly unnatural because forced upon us by heredity, environment, civilization in general. Therefore we must *look to earth* for our primary lesson in

Happiness. Before we can even picture Happiness to ourselves, we must revive the natural instinct that impels us to do and be the thing we love. Moreover, instead of making us ungodly, this return of spontaneity will put us in closer touch with the great celestial forces that come like a breath of wind, so fine and swift and gracious.

We call our dumb friends of the wood and air and sea the "lower animals." But in reality they are higher than we — because they are truer to what they know. In all the vital habits of life we must learn from them. Our food, our baths, our clothing, our exercise, our sleep and work and play must all conform to Nature if we are to be well, which is the first consideration in being happy.

This chapter is meant to be suggestive — nothing more. As a rule, the people who want most to be happy are the ones who think least. Hence the initial step is that of self-analysis; illustrations of method but not necessarily of conclusion are offered in this chapter. Whatever makes us true makes us happy; whatever makes us really happy must make us true; and the true thing is easier to find than the happy thing.

Happiness may come with a new frock, a business triumph, or a favorite amusement. And it may come with a mother's sacrifice, a nun's vow, or a martyr's anguish. It all depends on who we are, what we desire, how far we have gone in self-development.

Happiness is a power — not a possession. It is the capacity of being what we are, doing what we can, trusting in what we aspire to — and letting Providence take care of the rest. Every one may have it by working for it. And no one keeps it save as he earns more of it. For Happiness is not a gift, but a reward of merit.

The real secret of being happy is to be alert for new ways to grow. Joy is kaleidoscopic — a turn of the wrist and the combination changes. Every thought or act of ours puts a new set of forces into operation. If to-day we err, to-morrow we suffer. And we must learn to see the cause in the effect.

Moreover, the Happiness we sought may not satisfy us when it comes. We must reckon with the transformation of likes into dislikes, and dislikes into likes. Every moment of our lives, waking or sleeping, we are changing. What gave us pleasure yesterday may to-day bring sorrow. Like the flower, Happiness buds and blossoms and comes to fruition. Also like the flower, Happiness withers and falls away. Only the seed remains; which is the *aspiration at the heart of every joy*. If we are humanly wise, learning how to take this and plant it again, we can make of Happiness a perennial bloom, with a fruit to sustain us when the perfumed sensation of the petal has vanished into memory.

CHAPTER 11

Causes of Unhappiness

THE way to be happy is not to watch for Happiness, but to watch out for unhappiness.

Happiness should be to a human life what fragrance is to a rose, the murmur of winds to a wooded valley, the lap of the tide to a thirsty shore, or endless radiance to a sun fixed in glory. How does Happiness come? Not by any fixed human law, but streams and sings and shines through the very heart of us — without our knowing it. Finds us ready and suddenly takes possession!

When Nature speaks to us and we answer, when God moves through us and we act, then we are happy — happy and healthy. To be unhappy is always to be unhealthy. And that means not a quest but a cure. We restore health by cleansing the body of disease, we must restore Happiness in the same way.

To arrive at understanding of the matter, we may say that every soul bears to Happiness the relation that a window bears to light. You can darken a window in either of two ways — paint it black, or hide it in a dungeon. Likewise the human soul is darkened — by allowing false elements to gather on the surface, or by remaining in the prison-cell of ignorance. Nothing can make us unhappy but lack of self-knowledge or lack of faithfulness to that knowledge. When people or things cause misery, they do it by coming between us and Light. If we had always been true to our own instinct, reason, impulse, and aspiration, we should find unhappiness a physical, mental and moral impossibility. Therefore the clue to our problem is not so much "What will make us happy?" but rather "What could make us unhappy?"

The first, and most widespread, cause of unhappiness is our unjust habit of blaming others for the troubles that we brought upon ourselves. We stumble through life in the attitude of the rash child that bruises itself on a piece of furniture, then gets even by remarking "Naughty chair! I shall whip you!" Every ill that we meet we have walked into with our eyes open. If we did not see it, our spectacles were dusty — and that only proves we were lazy as well as impetuous.

Suppose, for instance, we "inherited" a bad temper, or a sluggish liver, or an extreme fondness for pleasure. Holding our ancestors responsible, we indulge the tendency, letting anger, or surliness, or sensuality, dominate our lives. Result: chronic unhappiness, due to chronic blindness. In a case of "bad heredity," there are two things to be said. First, the apparent evil is only a means to a larger good; second, every soul makes its own environment, consciously or unconsciously. Whatever we have is best — when we know how to use it. Anger is the vehicle of activity on a wrong road; and the way both to cure a temper and to get somewhere is to start our emotions going right. As for liver trouble, it usually occurs in people with a tendency to hasty and spasmodic action; the enforced lethargy being good for their peculiar temperament. Concerning pleasure, the desire for that is only the capacity of *feeling*, misplaced and misunderstood; take it from the senses and put it in the soul, then you have the quickest means to spiritual development. Some of the greatest evangels of history have been rioters in pleasure who turned their feeling heavenward instead of earthward.

These are but examples of this principle: *Every "handicap" in life is only a spur whose effect we have not yet discovered.* Whatever situation confronts us, it is the best possible for us at that particular time. Once realizing this, we cease to rebel.

Another cause of unhappiness is the idea of absolute dependence on some one thing to make us happy. If that goes, or fails to come, then we are in despair. No one thing can ever make us happy — we shall need as many things as we have powers to develop. The possession of rare books, lovely paintings, beautiful garments, rich viands, and congenial friends should make us happy; and equally should the lack of them. What we desire with the soul is already ours in effect, and can never be taken from us. But to want with the heart or the mind or the body is never to be satisfied and always to be restless. What we can lose we never owned. Disappointments come only to such as are undeveloped and need to be awakened. In short, the pleasure that turns to pain or privation has now lost its first incentive to make us grow. Therefore we should love its departing as once we loved its appearing.

Another cause of unhappiness is a confused relationship with Nature, self, the world, and God. Our habits of living should be wholly natural, but our motives for living wholly inspirational. Instead, our habits are generally artificial, our motives mechanical, and our lives a constant warfare between what we should like to do and what is expected of us. "Do the right thing and the world go hang!" is the wording on the sign-post that leads to Health and Happiness. The dread of seeming "queer" has kept more people from being themselves than any other vagary of the human mind. In the sight of both animals and angels, the queer people are the ones who are commonplace. Originality is the universal language of the soul. But we human midgets, with our near-sighted view of things, worship the conventionalized person whose instincts are dead, inspirations unborn, and emotions locked in a heart the keys of which now belong to Mrs. Grundy. Such a person can never enjoy life.

Happiness consists in possessing the body of an animal, the heart of a child, the brain of a man, the soul of a woman, and the consciousness of a god; then allowing each in turn to be lovingly exercised.

The forms and varieties of unhappiness are innumerable. But the only important thing to remember is that the cause and the cure lie in ourselves. If we cultivate the habit of looking back when trouble arises, we can soon acquire the vision to put our finger on the exact spot where we did what we knew we should not do, or failed to do what we knew we should. Then the way is clear.

The experienced physician knows that pain is a blessing in disguise, and that a visitation of minor ills generally ensures the patient against a long siege or a sudden death.

The same principle holds in the case of mental depression, emotional anxiety, or spiritual unrest. These conditions are to be welcomed as gracious and timely warnings of something wrong in the life. To be unhappy is merely to have broken some law of mental anatomy, emotional physiology, or spiritual hygiene.

First comes the diagnosis.

Roughly, we may classify all our troubles into four groups: Those pertaining to the body, the heart, the mind, and the soul. Oftentimes they overlap, sometimes they affect the entire being; but always the physical, emotional, mental and spiritual distinctions remain. A man with a perfect digestion cannot worry; and the man who does worry cannot digest; therefore the question is — How did the trouble start?

Right here is where general prescriptions for unhappiness mostly fail. They apply to *symptoms* instead of *causes*. There is no panacea for chronic unhappiness any more than for chronic headache. You cannot banish either except by removing the cause. Yet if you ask different authorities how to cure unhappiness, each will suggest a remedy so limited in application as to be of doubtful efficacy. Besought for a cure —

The minister answers, *"Pray."* Best for a doubting soul, perhaps for a weeping heart; but inadequate to relieve a food-poisoned body or to satisfy an undeveloped brain.

The educator answers, *"Read."* Likely to calm a perturbed mind, or equip an uninstructed body; but useless to aid a starved affection or bring back a lost ideal.

The physician answers, *"Exercise."* Fine to clear the brain as well as empower the physique; but helpless in the face of sorrow and absurd in the face of fear.

The business man answers, *"Work."* The best way to rout morbidity and prevent self-absorption; but empty of heart-interest and soul-advantage unless a great love prompts.

The politician answers, *"Fight."* Excellent for indecision, procrastination, self-sacrifice, and weakened vitality in certain temperaments; but nerve-destroying and soul-bearing.

The philanthropist answers, *"Give."* Antidote to greed, and panacea for indifference; but tending to emotional dissipation unless backed by cool judgment.

The reformer answers, *"Agitate."* Serving to impel action in those otherwise sluggish; but with anger and bitterness the only outcome until we turn to reforming ourselves.

The philosopher answers, *"Meditate."* Indispensable to poise amid the rush of our Western civilization; but solving no problem unless we live out the vision that silence affords.

The yogi answers, *"Renounce."* Makes one independent of the objects of desire and thus free of disappointment; but when carried too far, destroys life itself.

From this brief discussion we may draw the following conclusion:

The rational cure for unhappiness comprises two directions: *First, study out the cause in yourself; second, choose from the many prescriptions offered by authorities the one that your judgment indicates will do the work.* This is not the usual procedure. Wearing our heart on our sleeve, we invite the casual passer-by to stop and share our trouble. Consequence; we never get at the meaning of unhappiness, and we burden ourselves with a lot of advice that merely holds us back. All that makes unhappiness is our unhappy way of looking at it. The real trouble with most of us is that we haven't enough trouble to make us worth while. Many a poor slave or hopeless cripple has made of his life a beautiful song of thanksgiving to the God of Things as They Are. The purest song is that of suffering.

Not what comes, but how we take what comes, decides our Happiness.

With this principle firmly grounded, we simply do not care what comes. The weed of a moment trembles before the impending storm; the oak of a span of years lifts its head more proudly, then grips the earth with a new embrace of roots grown by the deluge. Blame God for the storm? Blame the weakling that cannot take what God sends to refresh the strong.

Neither fortune nor misfortune bears aught of good or ill; its character lies in our expectation and use. Weal and woe are interchangeable, at the option of ourselves. The virtue of a possession is in the power that earned it; the vice of a possession is in the weakness that squanders it, or the selfishness that hoards it. Love, the very scepter of Heaven, lifted Browning to the summit of bliss — and plunged Byron into gulfs of despair. Perhaps the reason we seldom gain just the thing we imagine we desire is that God saw it would only make us miserable. And *having worked* for it, we have secured the blessing of soul development.

A definition may be timely.

What is Fate, and to what degree responsible for human wretchedness? Our conception is that of a meddler, an ogre, a tyrant, or at best a merciless judge from whose decisions there is no appeal. In fact, however, the chief cause of human suffering is not Fate, but overwrought imagination. Fate is merely a gust of wind, that roguishly enters our domicile and puts things topsy-turvy for a couple of minutes. Papers on the floor, curtains awry, ink bottle tipsy, dust all over; and observing the wreckage we blame the wind. This isn't fair. We should have seen the storm coming, in time to shut the window. If we leave our mental parlor and emotional boudoir open to the passing breeze, what can we expect but a house in disorder?

We have clothed Fate with such a lot of imaginary power that she has grown to be almighty proud of nothing at all. Therefore it is a work of grace to dismiss her with a haughty "Poohpooh! You're nothing but an inconsequential atmospheric whiff!"

This attitude quickly delivers us from the odious presence. Because the one thing Fate cannot stand is being made fun of.

The crude analyses that follow may be suggestive; whether or not psychologically accurate, they tend to establish one principle: *The thing that makes us unhappy is something gone wrong in ourselves.*

And the way to recover peace of mind is to get acquainted with our own complex nature.

Envy is a mixture of weakness and rashness. When we look with envy at the automobile of our neighbor, it is not the machine we want but the sense of power that made it possible. If we had the power we should consider the possession a bauble — as he does. This much is certain; that what a man has earned he should keep, and what he has not earned he will not keep. For instance, automobile smash-ups are most often due to the carelessness of the "joy-rider," an employee of the owner with temporary use of the machine. The chauffeur has borrowed his master's car — and in it he comes to grief. If we could obtain our neighbor's possession without the poise that controls it — we should only destroy it and ourselves. But, in our weakness, we fall to the rash conclusion that laurels without a battle mean something. A rich man always hungers for something else, as we hunger for his possessions. We envy him, he envies us, and either would be more unhappy in the place of the other! What a ridiculous performance.

Jealousy is a mixture of aspiration and indolence. If the one we love cares for another, it is because the other wins respect or admiration by showing qualities that we have not developed. We wish we had; and we are jealous only so long as the wish remains inactive. Jealousy toward a rival ceases to exist from the moment we resolve to meet him in a fair fight. The stronger his attraction, the stronger our determination; and if we have the grit for a siege, we presently thank him for disclosing to our Loved One powers in us that were hidden before. A "fit of jealousy" is a confession of idealism thwarted by laziness or cowardice; make it a fight of emulation and the demons of anger will retire in disgust.

Suspicion is a mixture of dishonesty and fear. The youth who complains that his employer has favorites in the office, is the sort of person that watches the clock with one eye, the pay-envelope with the other, and has no eye left for his work. Being a robber, he expects to be robbed. A thousand mean employers could not keep a good man down; before he had the time to be hurt by meanness, his value would have reached the ears of somebody who did appreciate merit. Many a successful man has by sheer force of superiority created a place for himself where none was before.

Worry is a mixture of interference and irresponsibility. Interference with Nature, God or one's friend — and irresponsibility to one's self, occasion all the needless foreboding that keeps the worrier looking for troubles which never come. To worry over the past is to insult Nature — for Nature always does the best she can with the material at hand, every mistake being the effort of Nature to reach an ideal amid obstacles. To worry over the future is to insult God — for God has planned the future to perfect the past, and any change that we could make would only mar the whole. To worry over the present is to insult both our friend and ourselves — for if we are doing the next thing with promptness, thoroughness and skill, we have no time for anything but *constructive* work; also we enthuse our friend and put him at his best. In short, the cause of worry is a *lack in the worrier* — a lack of understanding, or of strength, courage, patience, or of scientific method. The cause of worry is never in the person or thing worried about.

If the business man torn with anxieties and depressed with financial burdens, would quietly force himself to look at things calmly, conserving his vitality and moving with poise, he would find such an attitude the most effective means of righting conditions. If the zealous mother, overanxious lest her children do wrong, or fretting because their will opposes hers, would stop and think that they are human beings whose highest function is not to obey another but to possess themselves, she would free the household from a despotism of petty human pride and allow both herself and her children to develop naturally into a mutual sympathy and trust. A worry is but an awakening in disguise; understood and heeded, it always opens the way to a blessing.

Loneliness is a mixture of super sensitiveness and artificiality. The plaint of being always misunderstood is uttered by those of too much feeling and too little depth. Physically, mentally, psychically, emotionally, every human being differs from every other. But spiritually, every two are the same. And often the very people who hold themselves most aloof, yearn most deeply for some one to understand and love them. We are so afraid of each other — with nothing to fear but the fear. Let a great strong magnetic personality enter a room filled with people — then see how the rest brighten up! The way to have a worldful of friends is to keep such a positive, buoyant, faith in Humanity that the surface shadows are melted by the light of understanding. Within the portal of the heart, the word "stranger" is unknown, the word "enemy" unthinkable. To be lonely is but to linger on the dim outer edge of one's self.

These illustrations, brief, inadequate, and possibly incorrect, serve but to show the true *method* of self-analysis.

What is the worst calamity? The failure of an ambition, the ruin of a home, the loss of a reputation, the pain of a lingering illness, the death of a loved one? *Not one of these woes but is kept alive by the way we nurse it.* Even the sorrow in death is that of blind selfishness — we bury our face in the shroud and think of what we shall miss, while the soul that was called beyond feels only the gain to us both. Sorrow comes to lift us out of the unrealities. And when we have taken our stand on the heights, we find again the loved one waiting — to whisper that there is no separation. Love, complete, grows immortal; only as we love in part are we bereft.

CHAPTER 12

How to Be Happy

THE perfect human life may be compared to a grand concert, wherein the chief parts are taken by a great organ and a fine quartette. The bass voice we call *Body*, the tenor we call *Mind*, the alto we call *Heart*, and the soprano we call *Soul*. The organ is Environment, the player is Civilization, and the leader of the choir is the Overbrooding Spirit.

It is the work of the organ to accompany — not to lead. And when we allow external forces to carry a tune of their own caprice, the result is a medley of deafening, discordant sound. The one supreme cause of unhappiness is our failure to make the world be still while we hearken to ourselves.

The melody of life, whatever it be, was meant for Soul to voice. And whenever Mind, or Heart, or Body assumes to take the place of Soul, the melody is in the wrong part, and the harmonic balance is destroyed. The problem of Happiness is the problem of training Mind, Heart, and Body to vibrate with Soul, then of bidding the world chime with the carol that God has given us each to sing.

First, then, we are to make these four voices as clear, strong and beautiful as we can. After that we shall need but to blend them. Happiness is the harmonious blending of all our powers, with the note of self-expression carried by each to the fullest.

HAPPINESS OF BODY

Happiness of body is found by going back to Nature. Whereas Happiness of Soul is found by going on to God. Happiness runs the gamut of Creation. To pause anywhere and imagine this the end is to decree one's self unhappy because unresponsive to the voice of guidance. We are animals that were — and we are gods to be. Neither despising our jungle-ancestry, nor doubting our heaven-estate, we shall be happy in finding who and what we are, then being just that. The great human kill-joy is the conventional habit of *pretending*, to the world and one's self. The divinest gift is that of being natural.

It is a matter of history that the following means, and others like them, have restored Happiness to bodies weak or ailing; and have also maintained vigor in bodies firm and buoyant. This is not a medical treatise. But we cannot get anywhere worth reaching unless we start with the body.

1. *Eat simply and rationally.* Probably half of the foods on American dining-tables are unfit to eat. Consequence; the malady of this nation is nervous dyspepsia. If we used the common sense in feeding ourselves that we do in feeding horses, we could work like horses, and never complain. The natural foods of man are fruits, vegetables,

cereals, nuts, perhaps also eggs and meat. The natural meal hour is when we are hungry — and not any other time. The natural number of meals is two a day. The natural method of eating is by slow mastication, that the taste of each morsel may be fully enjoyed; and with no idea of false hospitality mixed up in mind or stomach. Also the natural function of eating is to keep us immune to all forms of disease. Compare the natural with the actual — then you have the clue to physical unhappiness. Rational salvation starts in the stomach.

2. *Learn to relax.* Much of the worry, confusion and irritability of American life is but a thoughtless habit of tension, that accomplishes nothing. The energy we waste could, if wisely directed, bring us anything on earth. Just a few minutes every day of perfect quiet, with nerves, muscles, senses, even thoughts, put to sleep by our will, is sufficient to rejuvenate the body. The most advantageous time is that following the noon luncheon or late breakfast.

3. *Stand straight and breathe to the bottom of your lungs.* The poise erect is the poise efficient. When we are ill or despondent, we sag. But when we sit up and look the world in the face, we automatically generate vim, courage, endurance, self-respect. Never mind if somebody calls out "Chesty." Napoleon was chesty. And he conquered while he stayed so. In the breath-box lies power. Get it out.

4. *Hit the game harder.* The mental resolution to win at all hazards becomes a great elixir for the body. When the spirit of conquest dies out, the proof is not of increasing wisdom but of encroaching age. The youth's ideal of a superb athletic champion should hold throughout life; when we cease to exult in physical prowess, we cease to convey our fullest spiritual potency. The natural man is product of the chase primeval; the subliminal man is producer of a calm eternal; between the two must the evolutional man, the man of to-day, wisely alternate, to keep a sane working balance. But most of us are nearer the elemental; and to that we must be true.

5. *Work up a good sweat.* After a Turkish bath, you breathe more freely; when you exercise the lungs to the fullest, you waken the solar plexus; when you have a warm, vivid, sympathetic solar plexus, you make way for the immortal ego to reach the outer world; therefore so crude and common a thing as a vapor-box enhances ethereal growth. A wood-pile, however, is better than a lazy thermal cabinet. Rig up a home gymnasium and see how many kinds of fun it is.

6. *Laugh at the weather.* A healthy anatomy enjoys all seasons alike. The only frown a storm should occasion would be that of hating the conventions that prevented our splashing in it. If you never breasted a March gale in a spirit of dauntless challenge, you have missed a real pleasure intended by Nature for all her children. Regarding sunstroke, that is principally anxiety on top of undigested food; there is no condition of weather which is aught but advantageous if we know how to meet it.

7. *Ponder on the habits of animals in the wild.* This topic would require a volume, to elaborate the principle. Here we only suggest that the untamed creatures of the forest, hill and stream, might, if they could speak, establish colleges of hygiene and therapeutics, whereat the wisest man would have to matriculate as a primary scholar. Animals know how to live, being taught of Nature. Humans do not know, having deserted Nature; and as the only other master of the subject is God, we must reach the stature of angels before we recover the wisdom we have lost.

8. *Revel in earth, air, water, and sun.* Find the magic in the touch of Mother Earth. Whenever it is possible, lie flat on the dry grass for hours at a time, absorbing magnetism in every starved cell. Cultivate a hobby that takes you out-of-doors. While there is work to do, alone, in chamber or study, wear as few clothes as provide comfort — the effect of sunlight and breeze on the whole organism is both soothing and tonic, certain health institutions being founded on the principle of the air bath. Finally, investigate the cold-water ablution on rising

as a part of the day's regime; if the plunge is too severe, there are milder forms with equal power to set us a-tingle. All that the body of us wants is to keep in touch with the elements that gave it birth. And a careful study of Naturist philosophy will amply repay one in saving of doctor's bills.

HAPPINESS OF HEART

Happiness of heart is measured by how fully we can love, asking no return, and thinking not to possess. There are two kinds of Heart-misery; that from shutting affection out, and that from hoping to make it *all* of life. There are many who steel themselves against emotion — and they shrivel into walking mummies. There are some who lavish themselves in love, adoration, service — and the only reward is a broken heart to bind and lay away. A very few have learned the secret of Heart-happiness; which is to *love and let go!* Whoever belongs to us cannot go, whoever does not belong should never have come.

1. *Refuse to be disappointed.* Whatever happens, might have been worse. And it will grow better as fast as we consider it good. Looking back over the years, we can always reflect that our sorrows were only blessings in disguise. If we could realize this in the midst of our tears, we could smile now as we shall smile later. Seeing the lesson in what comes when it comes; that is a boon worth coveting. The heart of everything, and everybody, is good. To find the heart is to be happy. Meanwhile it may be a relief — as every woman knows, to let down the flood-gates and

2. *Have a "good cry."* In this foolish world of repression and misunderstanding, the pent-up feelings, of joy or anguish, that gather day by day must have outlet or become intolerable. Just to sweep away the surface unrealities and restore a larger vision, a blinding flood of tears proves a comfort. As a mere physical relief, wise physicians

encourage in their patients the timely expression of emotion. And the spiritual gain is even greater.

3. *Share somebody's trouble.* This usually scatters our own. Because, most likely, the friend is braver than we would be — and that makes us ashamed. Also we forget to be selfish. And sorrow is always selfish.

4. *Confess your faults.* To the Great Father, or to a minister, or to a loved one. A friend is one who sees us perfect until we must become so. And confessing to a friend is like polishing a mirror until it reflects without blur. The object of repentance is not self-reproach but self-encouragement. Just to close the door in the twilight, and whisper, to the one who understands, how honestly we tried though we failed, is to go forth a giant in spiritual strength, with armor of faith invincible.

5. *Count your "mercies."* A fine practice on Thanksgiving morning is to call the family together, distribute pencils and paper, then offer a prize for the child who has the most blessings written down. He really gets two prizes, because the ability to see a blessing is reward enough in itself. If we count up, we shall probably find that our joys outnumber our miseries about fifty to one. And that one will lead to a joy if we follow its guidance.

6. *Cultivate a healthy sense of humor.* The best antiseptic for the emotions is the habit of smiling at ourselves. And if we can't smile — smile because we can't. Overseriousness propagates disease-germs at an alarming rate. And a hearty laugh is the best germ-killer imaginable. A very few tears will drown an atom; and we are all atoms. Spiritually we are the suns and stars of the future; physically, mentally, morally, we are for the present mere grains of sand. Should a mite take on the airs, or the worries, of a mammoth? The funniest thing to behold is the heirloom quilt of patchwork-importance wherein some folks array themselves and think they are dressed for company. For a man or woman to feel egotistical or personally momentous, is about as rational as for a tumble-bug to fall into a crown and announce itself king.

7. Form a habit of anonymous giving. Two things mar the beauty of a gift: First, a knowledge of its money-value; second, a feeling of obligation to the giver. The way to prevent such a misfortune is to let the giver be nameless. In short, play Santa Claus. The real untruth in a Christmas celebration is when Dear Santy puts away his fairy garb. Kindness should be as free as light; and if we notice the channel through which it comes, there must be cloudiness. Is there a greater joy than to walk through the hovel-district of a crowded city, your arms heaped with flowers for the wistful, eager, beauty-starved children? What they know you by is a fragrant memory. Could a name achieve such immortality?

8. Keep busy. Brooding is chiefly idling. Of itself, hope returns with action. The cure for a lost affection is to lack time to hunt for it. Moreover, sentiment to be kept solid must have sand mixed with it. What crushes the dreams of our youth is our own lack of grit before the inevitable world-impact. Not our friendship with fairies makes us impractical, but our enmity with facts.

When the spirit of our dream takes full possession of us, we could face ten thousand hells with the power of a hurricane. We never feel too much, we feel too little for the will to be charged and the brain quickened. The masters of the world have been men who were all feeling, but who put it where they wanted it, and did with it as they chose. Nothing satisfies in the end but work; regular, systematic, ordinary, *work with a great love back of it and greater purpose ahead.* A dream is justified by drudgery alone; and drudgery must be sanctified through dreaming.

HAPPINESS OF MIND

Happiness of mind accrues chiefly from *independent* thinking. Souls like Newton, Spencer, Agassiz and Ibsen take their keenest pleasure in following an original thought to its logical end. To them, the physical sensation of developing unused brain cells affords the same delight that common people realize through taste, or hearing, or some other external medium. The majority feel right but think wrong: and the minority who think right usually feel wrong. So to be happy throughout, we must share the instinct of the masses but exercise our own intellect. For example; many a college professor has for a wife a social butterfly. He tries to get all his Happiness through his books, while she tries to get all hers through her parties. If she would study, her delight in people would be more intense; and if he would play, his grasp of principles would be more convincing. Each by limiting the sphere of Happiness, lessens the force. Misery is but the mold on a stagnant mind.

In mental exuberance the prime factor is freedom to think for one's self. No physical joy approaches the ecstasy of the poet, the inventor, philosopher, who has fearlessly pursued an idea into realms unknown, and after many a bruise has captured the winged thing in his fine-spun net of imagination.

When the autumn wind sighs through the treetops, the fireside group in their cheerful housing pity the lonely huntsman; but he, absorbed in the glee of the chase, forgets the existence of them that pity. In the forest of Truth none are ever lost but they who pause to be lonely; for never till then does the golden glint on the wings of the vision cease to point the way.

The following lines of suggestion may open avenues to pleasures for the intellect.

1. *Discredit public opinion.* The average person is a child emotionally and spiritually; so their united judgment reveals the immaturity of a child — without the saving spontaneity. Yet if the multitude and ourselves disagree, we doubt ourselves and follow the crowd because it is a crowd. This is intellectual bondage; and slaves are not happy. A wrong idea that we own is better than a right one that we

borrowed. And the giants of history have been men and women who dared say what they thought, despite the snarl of the mob. Emerson the people called crazy, Napoleon they ridiculed, Luther they fought, Columbus they branded a witless adventurer, Wagner they hounded from place to place, Lincoln they blackguarded, Jesus they crucified. Yet these lonely figures, robbed of appreciation, were to be envied — not pitied. For they stood on the horizon, looking through their dream down the vista of the ages. And to be able for that is to exult.

2. *Get an ambition that spans earth and sky.* The power to think big is of itself a joy unconfined. What do most of our thoughts, our words, our deeds, really signify? Nothing but wasted energy and lost opportunity. A fixed purpose to own a bootblack shop is more commendable in the sight of Heaven than a shilly-shally hope to reform the world. The great insult to God is an aimless existence. Yet the rich, so many of whom are guilty, wonder why their wealth fails to make them happy. Any ragged boy may think himself a millionaire; and that is more fun than being it — unless you keep the child imagination to show you how to spend the money.

3. *Surround yourself with what you want to be.* It is the power of ideation that has grown men out of animals and will grow gods out of men. Each human resolve is photographed in Heaven, to be developed by Father Time according to the clearness of impression. We cannot escape doing, having, being, the thing we desired. Most of our wishes are confused in our own mind — hence they fail of accomplishment. Take the matter of health, for example. Many of us know chronic health-seekers who suppose that all they need to be perfectly happy is to be well. They deceive themselves. What they are really after is pity, or attention; self-will, self-indulgence, irresponsibility; or some other hindrance to health. Chronic disease is fundamentally a moral issue.

To be well, be with well people. Do as they do, think as they think, talk as they talk, feel as they feel; join their games, contests, amusements; share their abundant joy of living; match their wits and rival their ambitions; be absolutely positive as they are, even a bit conceited; in short, borrow the action and the atmosphere of health until you can make your own. Or if you want to be happy, make friends with jolly people; read funny books; eat the smile off the breakfast-food advertisement — the way to preserve the smile is not to eat the food; go to humorous plays — the polite endeavor to laugh will afford strenuous exercise to the risibles; look pleased at yourself in the mirror whenever you pass that way — a look-ing-glass is the most appropriate thing in the world to laugh at; in short, purloin a grin that you can wear until it blossoms naturally.

4. *Master the art of concentration.* The supreme intellectual delight is to think so hard that the heavens might fall unobserved. Also, that is how to win. When a shrewd man is intent on a business problem or line of action, he unconsciously frowns. That proves him happy; for the brain most enjoys a knotty, twisty, ugly proposition. Masters of finance are but ordinary men who have learned how to think through the difficulties that surrounded them. And the exhilaration of the game itself, not the ease of their marble palace, becomes the everlasting lure.

5. *Play fair.* This refers not alone to honesty, but primarily to our feeling toward the other fellow. A decided mental uplift comes from viewing our opponent with the same generosity that we show to ourselves. Tolerance should be used for the way it helps the user. Everybody sees things from where he happens to stand. If a Baptist and a Catholic had changed roads, they would have changed religions. The only cure for prejudice is to move on, this affliction being a form of mild paralysis. Those who habitually suspect the motives of others are themselves intellectually muscle-bound; which condition scarcely makes for being happy.

6. *Balance employment and amusement.* This means: a professor of mathematics should not play chess for enjoyment, nor a hod-carrier play baseball. A natural instinct for all-roundness should lead the professor to take boxing lessons, while the laborer grew expert in mastering Robert Browning. A variation of this principle would be for the desk worker to make a habit of standing on the car platform to and from his office, tensing his muscles and breathing for all he's worth; while the ditch digger on the same car was busying himself with a book.

7. *Do something different.* Monotony deadens the brain more than all other causes put together. Just having to be angels would make us diabolic. And the curse of unbroken routine changes many a heavenly disposition into a nonheavenly temper. Run away some time and tell not a soul where you're going; or lie in bed a whole day when you aren't sick and don't have to; or borrow a neighbor's child and hasten to the circus, relieved of the hang-dog look; or seek a generous roof in a large, emphatic desert and then just holler — plain holler. Every healthy child at a ballgame would love to be the megaphone man. And grown-ups can do no better than emulate the feeling of a normal child.

8. *Study the teachings of other nations.* The Persians, the Japanese, or the East Indians, often exercise more philosophy in a day than many of us learn in a lifetime. Of the subjective powers, which are the vital ones, we remain in gross and lamentable ignorance. When we discover that the principles of our boasted "New Thought" were known and lived thousands of years ago, some of them by races we imagined semi-barbarian, all of a sudden our pride gets a shock. Too many of us Americans are infants in real wisdom. And the sooner we appreciate the fact, the sooner our heads will manifest a normal, healthy, happy size.

HAPPINESS OF SOUL

Happiness of Soul is attained through discerning and removing all that is not Soul. Then the consciousness of immortality awakens, a sense of power illimitable thrills the whole being, a beautiful peace descends like a dove, and we know that from the beginning all is right with the world. This larger vision may come through sorrow, meditation, self-sacrifice, worship, love, or any other crisis of experience that lifts us, momentarily, from the tangled mesh of human relationship.

In the spiritual world, duty and ecstasy are one. They should be one in the material world, the wrongful separation of them has robbed spirituality of its natural winsomeness. Soul-vision promises, not cheerless deprivation, but human joy intensified. There is nothing we really love on earth but we shall love more in Heaven.

When Body and Soul are attuned, neither can enjoy without the other. And if either fails to enjoy, the other should be questioned. The one word portending rapture complete is: *Clarify*. When we have learned to distinguish between the *race-thought of surface pleasure* and our own *feeling of inner Happiness*, most of the things we struggle to obtain will have ceased to allure.

Soul's first mandate is: *Enjoy all things more*. Enjoy so much that the object of desire is melted in the pure light of devotion, and only the essence remains. Enjoy pain; for the lesson it brings. Enjoy privation; for the purpose it strengthens and the freedom it ensures. Enjoy sorrow; for the way it relieves us of out-grown possessions. Enjoy failure; for the road it opens to success. Enjoy misunderstanding; for the sympathy it yields with our fellows. Enjoy martyrdom; for the power it gives to see the world as nothing, and the transport of soul out of flesh. Happiness, in the end, is to reject Happiness, and to live, or die, for Truth.

Soul finds Happiness in two ways: by *seeing* with infinite clearness, then *doing* with infinite strength. Soul must fight to keep its "illusions" — those beautiful dreams of childhood that came from the heart of God; Soul must work in the treadmill — for there the soulless, bound, cry for a glimpse beyond; Soul must exult in travail — for to create is the sum of earth's anguish and ecstasy; Soul must persevere to the end of time, aloof and supreme, caring not if Heaven or if Hell be the path; soul must do whatever seems hardest, thereby to glory in its own divine strength. Soul understands both the longing for Happiness and the danger in seeking it for itself. Happiness lies ever in some new turn of the road to Perfection; and we stumble if we look too far ahead. Soul would just fill the crisis of the moment, lavishing itself on the need of the world. And when the Great Spirit takes possession, working without hindrance through the mortal, the unsought but sure reward is bliss.

Life is a wonderful symphony, quivering with joy to the ear that knows music. If the instrument of self be attuned, and the player understands harmony, there is never any doubt of the Leader, or question if the melody be true. To listen low, and catch but a strain from the Song of the Ages; then to lift the tune as best we may; that is to be happy as the angels are — and as men should be.

"Evil is hard to bear, and doubt is slow to clear
    Each sufferer says his say, his scheme of the weal and woe;
But God has a few of us whom He whispers in the ear —
    The rest may reason and welcome! 'Tis we musicians *know*."

Deep in the heart of the bird, the flower, the poet, and the child, lies that mystic, fragile, fleeting thing called Happiness. Perhaps after all it is only the power to sense the ideal, share the invisible, grasp the intangible, and build a new world from the same dream-dust God used when He fashioned this.

HEALTH EFFICIENCY GAUGE

(FOR GENERAL DETERMINATION OF THE HEALTH PROBABILITIES OF A
NORMAL INDIVIDUAL)

*DIRECTIONS. Where the following items have been made a part of your
health equipment, place the numeral 5 in blank space opposite. Add numerals
for your health efficiency grade.*

1. Freedom from pain, weakness, and all
   fear of disease _____

2. Vigorous belief that it is vastly better to
   prevent disease than to wait to cure it _____

3. Choice, amount and time of meals based on
   hunger alone _____

4. Average bedtime ten o'clock, and fifty-six
   hours of sleep a week _____

5. Daily exercise in open air, and enjoyment
   of same _____

6. Thoro perspiration at least once a week _____

7. Morning bath, with brisk rub following _____

8. Summer vacation where swimming,
   boating, tramping, etc., available _____

9. Cultivation of a garden, if only in
   backyard _____

10. All clothing made loose and comfortable,
    hygienic before stylish _____

11. Windows in home and office never entirely closed _____

12. Habit of deep, slow, diaphragmatic
    breathing _____

13. Correct posture while sitting, standing, walking _____

14. Frequent air and sun baths _____

15. Sanitary methods and appliances where you live and where you work _____

16. Knowledge of mental and spiritual factors in health _____

17. Examination by physician, dentist, oculist, once a year at least, for signs of warning _____

18. Independence of all health fads or cults _____

19. Refusal to worry over anything _____

20. Absorbing interest in your work _____

_____

NOTE. This Gage does not include the mention of particular symptoms, because their discovery and treatment belong in the realm of the physician.

Total equals general percentage of your health status. It should be 80, tho the average is probably not over 35.

CHAPTER 13

Enjoying Ourselves

THERE is a magic of Happiness — the magician's name is *Fun*. Any child will tell you this; and if you haven't a child to teach you things, you will soon become very stupid. Only children know the freshness and the ardor, the lure and thrill and witchery of Happiness. By instinct they enjoy themselves to the full, making life a game and their chosen leader *Fun*. Keeping their spirit is the surest way to be happy.

Work may lead to Happiness — after long, dull years of slaving in a treadmill of routine.

Study may lead to Happiness — through deep fogs of speculation, mists of doubt, and shadows of external authority.

Pain may lead to Happiness — with a line of ugly scars to show where we fell, and a memory seared by anguish and bitterness.

Other things may lead to Happiness — at a cost that few are willing to pay.

But Fun leads to Happiness here and now, and we enter easily by the wide, sunny portal of the gracious child-heart. Is not the child-heart a miracle in itself; what other door is both clear as crystal and stanch as iron? When we have wandered in later years and the door closes, we stoutly boast (with a secret sigh) that we have at last grown practical — they aren't any such things as fairies. While the fairies, meeting as always in their safe shining palace of the wondrous child-heart, mourn us among the dead.

I think we *are* dead, when we find ourselves barred from the councils of the fairies. The moment we are quite grown-up we begin to die bodily. This is plain physiology — no poetry whatever; ask any doctor. Being grown-up is the universal misfortune; staying childlike is the rare fate given to those who earn it by open-mindedness. Pity the child who has outgrown its parents; pity more the parents who have outgrown their child.

Enjoying ourselves is being childlike. How do I know? Anybody knows, who hasn't turned mummy. There are some unfortunate people with a petrified backbone, anesthetic brain and hyperacidulated stare who imagine that being dignifiedly aged is the whole end of human existence. To such laggards of the tomb a whistling boy is anathema in extremis. Being half-dead, they assume to judge life. Such folks are usually very rich, or very highly educated; their natural selves have been smothered in veneer. Money and mind both kill what they cover. Living is *feeling*, and the man ashamed of sentiment or the woman afraid of emotion stands in the shadow of death. We are none of us educated, none of us prepared to live, until we have zealously gone to school to children.

Are the pleasures and amusements of Society good or bad? What effects do our own recreations have on our life, work, happiness and character? Is the choice and amount of play a real factor in growth and efficiency? *Ask the children.* Life is only play to children; life would be only play to men and women if men and women kept as wise as children.

There is a test for pleasure whose application is universal. It takes the form of a double query: *"Do children like it,* and would *you let them have it?"* If they like it, it is more or less natural; if you would let them have it, it is more or less divine. Do they like champagne suppers, problem plays, men's all-night "smokers," and women's scandal-parties? Then such things are not natural. Would you share them with children? If not, then they are not desirable or divine. Acquired tastes are mostly bad. And the pleasures you have to learn to like are perils in disguise.

Never was a false teaching falser than the current opinion that some enjoyments are for grown people only, because grown people are worldlywise. What is not good for your child is less good for you. The baby is protected from seeing wrong by the radiance of its dream-vision; while the baby's parents, unless they are mystics to the death, have allowed themselves to be robbed of the halo that encircles all those of sure discernment. Parents read books to see if the pages are fit for children — it might well be the other way 'round! Children are safe till men make them coarse and women make them foolish.

How can little folks teach us the full art of enjoying ourselves?

Let us watch and find out.

Children have a real play-hunger. This is as necessary to health as an appetite for meals. Play is to the emotions what food is to the muscles; without it they starve. Now the emotions are the muscles of the psychic organism; by means of them we grasp and use the vital principles that shape our lives. Hence the need for emotions that are well fed and regularly exercised. When you see a lot of happy children playing on the sidewalk, what do you feel like doing? Banishing them, with a scolding? Then you are a psychic paralytic. Or getting down in the midst of them, loosening your dignity, limbering your creaking joints, lopping off your absurd cares and picayunish worries? Then you are a psychic athlete.

Children need few things, outside of themselves. Blind-man's buff, leap-frog, and pussy-wants-a-corner, these typical childish games require no studied rehearsal, no costly paraphernalia. We are a long way from the natural, my friends. And we shall find our lives more keenly enjoyable to the extent that we rid ourselves of the useless trappings and anxious conventions of play. Skipping stones on a duck-pond, or walking a rag baby up and down stairs, is more fun to the kiddies than all our labored amusements are to us. We ought to be ashamed of ourselves, for the dull and deadly intricacy that we have woven into the simple joys of comradeship.

Children prove the democracy of play. Unless they have been twisted by their elders (and worsers), 'Rastus Johnsing and Reginald Knick-erbocker play marbles, side by side, to their heart's supreme content. If 'Rastus has no collar — Reginald has no contempt. If Reginald has no picturesque vocabulary — 'Rastus has no pride in sharing his. They are pals. Thirty years later, how often does Reginald acknowl-edge a 'Rastus, a 'Rastus approve a Reginald? (The approval is worth more.) The ugly barrier of caste has been formed, and the splendid humanness of childhood forgotten. One is a "high-brow," the other a "low-brow" — what superficial things men call each other! The place to measure a man is not where he wears his hat but where he wears his smile. Wisdom welcomes everybody.

Children know how to relax. Whereas grownups rest so hard that they're all tired out with the effort. In New York City, of a summer time, Monday morning is the tiredest morning in the week. A large proportion of our estimable citizens have jaunted Coney Island-ward and have pushed so fast to get their nickel's worth of fun that the competition is well-nigh fatal. If any youngsters were along, they promptly went to sleep on the way home, the rest of the party not having sense enough to depart when departure fell due. This is the age of nervous troubles, because this is the age of artificial pastimes. Play is the scientific mode of relaxation. And if you are afflicted with too many "nerves," you can profitably study boys and girls in the recess-hour at school.

Children make play out of work. They resemble animals in this respect. Do flowers, bees and birds take vacations in order to enjoy life? Play should be only a different kind of pleasure from work. No amount of recreation will atone for a disagreeable occupation. Give a normal child something to do and he first looks for a way to make it easy and pleasant. But to men work is too often either an ecstasy of genius or a monotony of despair — neither being permanent or sane. Grown-ups need a Froebel more than youngsters ever did. For in all our greatest achievements no motive could be better than the fresh, clean, earnest, honest spirit of the game — the everyday spirit of childhood.

Children are whole-souled. And that is the secret of Happiness. Pleasure is delightful because we throw our whole selves into it. Whenever duties equally absorb us, they too become joyous. It is the reservations and repressions of life that cause the misery. When we open our hearts to each other and give ourselves a chance to be real, the doubts and perplexities vanish, the griefs take wing, the weaknesses turn into powers for good. To those who charge all their activities with the deepest feelings of their nature, life is just one long play-day, while still a work-day.

CHAPTER 14

Ought To Versus *Want To*

WHICH of these warring elements will produce Happiness? Neither — and both. Neither alone — both together.

That word "versus" should be stricken from the language. It doesn't belong. It's a lie. Without warning or provocation, it has made foes out of friends and corpses out of foes. Foemanry is a species of hallucination, brought upon us by the artificiality in which we live undiscovered to ourselves. You can't fight with a man you know. Enemies are but strangers with their names torn off. Their disability came before the battle.

Ought-To and *Want-To* are twins. And they look so much alike you can scarcely tell one from the other. This may not appear all at once — because these mischievous twins have been wearing false faces. *Ought-To* wore a face as long as a clothes-pin, *Want-To* wore a face as round as an apple. They did it to please their friends. Very good people — the kind that worship *Ought-To*, aren't usually happy unless they're mournful; whereas very joyous people — the kind that chum with *Want-To*, aren't really good unless they're happy.

So the twins, to keep their followings, had to choose each a mask with a human failing in it. Idolatry is always the worship of a mask. Let us now strip the guise from our idols and view them as they are. Whether Puritan or Sybarite, we have patterned our lives not by the whole truth but by a kink in our temperament. Neither Duty nor Inclination can be a safe guide until each makes us know and love the other.

In almost every community, there are two welldefined sets of people — the good ones proud of their uppishness, and the bad ones proud of their offishness. Now the character that a man is proud of he has usually pawned for a reputation; and if he steps too high he's going to lose the ticket. Goodness never poses; and when Badness turns a deaf ear, it is that something else is masquerading under the name of Goodness.

Righteousness can not be wholly good, for it is not wholly happy. Nor can Wickedness be wholly bad, for it is not wholly miserable. Throughout the everlasting struggle of Good and Evil, both contestants are half-blind; the churchgoer in his *devotion to false* duties, the pleasureseeker in his *denial of real* duties. Not with our conscience do we fight our neighbor, but with our substitute for a conscience. Our conscience is never aware that our neighbor exists.

Can you imagine the sunshine quarreling with a flower? Yet if the sun and the blossom were human, each would say to the other, "You are doing wrong because you don't do as I do." And each would imagine itself a paragon of virtue for having thus questioned the virtue of its neighbor! There is probably nothing so stupid in the Universe as a very good person who has not yet learned to think. He himself creates much of the evil by seeing evil where evil is not.

This whole conflict between so-called Virtue and so-called Vice resolves to a grapple in the dark of *unreal duties* with *unreal desires*. All unpleasant things are unreal things. And the great secret of enjoying life is to have so clear a vision that what we should do and what we would do are always interchangeable. We cannot really want the thing but what is best for us. Knowledge of, and faith in, our own supreme desire will be found the boulevard to Heaven. Any other path leads roundabout, into thickets, over crags, along great sloughs of despond. The man whose only guide is Duty could never be happy in Heaven — even if he reached there.

The principal vice of the very dutiful is that they are also very direful. The reason is apparent; they have so bound up their conscience with a tapeline whereby to measure their neighbors that the poor thing can't breathe. A healthy conscience laughs — it is the ailing one that groans. No mirror betrays so much as a mournful countenance, a pessimist being a fellow who has got an unexpected view of his own insides.

May not doing right and frowning be as irreligious as doing wrong and smiling? Is it natural to be morally stiff-necked? Who first dared assume that Righteousness is repellent? Not Goodness is unpopular, but Goodness with a grouch. And the grouch came from something that was not good.

The next vice of the very dutiful takes the form of hallucination. They suppose that we ought to be commonplace, that our thought, feeling, speech, action and hope of salvation should precisely tally with that of John Smith next door, or that of Lady Genevieve Knickerbocker over on the avenue. The styles in virtue are what make virtue vicious. A life can be judged by its motive alone — and who sees that but God? We seldom do right altogether until we do something that looks wrong to other people. Why? Because to the majority anything different is questionable. And when we become ourselves, we are altogether different. The soul is without pattern, the soul must create anew.

Another vice of the very dutiful — perhaps the most grievous one — is that of cowardice. They are good because they want to go to Heaven, and they fear the consequences of being bad. Is not this a paltry state of mind? A larger nobility looms in the splendid daring of a pirate chief! The courage to risk all on the venture we love most proves how close we are to the Power that moves the world. Results are the measure of weaklings, actions the measure of men.

Is it right? Then do it. Forget Heaven, forget Hell, forget the world and go ahead. Fear punishment? No. Expect reward? No. Ask advice? No. Get clear, then realize the divinity of abandon. The purpose of conscience is not to restrain but to inspire, uplift, impel. "Thou Shalt Not" is but a poor translation of "Thou Canst and Wilt!" One positive desire contains more religion than do a million negative duties. Instinct is a duty, impulse a duty, emotion a duty, ambition a duty, kindness a duty, sympathy a duty, independence a duty. These are duties because they were desires. A duty is a desire with a fence around it. All that most people see is the fence, whereas they should first look for the flowers inside.

What makes Right wrong and Wrong right is our external standard of right and wrong. We impose, on ourselves and our neighbors, duties that have no excuse for being save the excuse of antiquity. Most of our duties are but the customs of our friends whitewashed by our own conscience.

Our social duties, what are they? To be thoughtful, generous, patient, calm, loving; to see good in every one, and feel how the world is a vast brotherhood of souls marching Heavenward. But to follow any such program is to annihilate the social code. With artificial graces the gods of hospitality, who can be friendly in a simple, honest way? Instead, we figure on the cost of our entertainments, striving to awe our guests and eclipse that function at Mrs. Montmorency Jones's last week. We pay calls and are glad if the callee is out. We are nice to the members of "our crowd," and over-nice to the people in the set just above us — as though friendship were a matter of brownstone and livery! We condemn the anarchist and spurn the Ishmaelite; yet these virtual outcasts, hunting some way to be honest with themselves, may teach us the first lesson of altruism, that the duty most friendly is to shape our own character in view of the others.

Our intellectual duties, what are they? To think originally, plan definitely, execute wisely; and be ever alert for the coming of a new truth in unsuspected guise. But how can we judge clearly when we have filled our brains with gossip, anxiety, complaint, mean stories and newspaper trash? The human brain is the rag bag of civilization. And until we empty it of the wornout articles that other people have jammed in it, we need not expect to have a place for our jewels. Crystals do not gather in the midst of cobwebs.

Our financial duties, what are they? To make money, save it, and give it, all three. The capitalist, the miser, and the spendthrift, is each a third of a man. Nor will each grow complete by denying the value of the others. Here again we allow popular opinion to influence us wrongly. We attribute unselfishness to the pauper, and greed to the millionaire; whereas the pauper's covetous eying of the pennies demonstrates not only greed but sloth. No man has found himself until the work he is doing pays him well. Nature is lavish with all her children; when we skimp, we disobey. If life is good, the larger living the better life.

Our religious duties, what are they? To know God's plan for the world, and to embody our own highest ideal. This means a faith unconquerable, a hope serene and steadfast, a joy that lifts the veil from sorrow and triumphs even in the grave! What if the vision come through public worship, or silent meditation, or the human leading of a sympathetic hand? God has so many ways of approach that even the atheist may be nearing Heaven by a path which the minister has not seen. Not how often we go to church, not how much we give to missions, not how fully we have memorized the Bible; but how deeply we love our neighbor, and how far we radiate the light of our own soul; this declares the spirit of God within us.

As much could be told of the unreal desires as of the unreal duties.

But the dutiful people have held themselves patterns for all the world; and a pattern becomes ragged much sooner than the article by which it is cut. Reform is the height of human presumption; God wants men made after Himself, not after other men. The sinner has been lectured enough, it is time that we lectured the saint. The saint must teach the sinner how to want things *better* — but the sinner must teach the saint how to want things *more*. A duty apart from a desire is the shell of a nut apart from the kernel. Some good may be had from an unreal desire, but to an unreal duty there is only waste.

This plea is not for the abolition of conscience, but for the recognition and extension of it through all the departments of life. To many people, conscience has become a faded bookmark in some historic tome of shelved and musty morals. Conscience must be lifted bodily from the dimethical alcove in which it somehow got buried, and be firmly established in the ordinary lives of everyday folks. Conscience belongs in the physical senses, in hunger and thirst, in energy and magnetism, in the desire for work and play, in the choice of companions, in the ordering of the day's routine, in the feeling, thought and word of the passing moment, in the ambition of the morrow, in the yearning to love and give' and serve, in every least expression of a human life. In short, the purpose of conscience is to tell us what we want, why we need it, how to get it.

Thus the Happiness of doing right is only the Happiness of being real. Realness is Tightness; and the man who desires powerfully enough, clearly enough, kindly enough, does his duty without knowing it. A duty is not a duty until we call it something else.

IV. RELATIONSHIPS

CHAPTER 15

Bravery, Breadth, Brotherhood

GEOGRAPHY has little to do with where we live.

What fixes our abode is the realm of thought, feeling, purpose, decision, action, in which we consciously move toward an infinite destiny ever receding, ever expanding, ever entrancing with hope of itself.

We may dwell in the same house all our lives — and a new world for every year.

We may do the same thankless work day after day buoyed with a hope immortal and the endless joy of betterment — or we may flit from pleasure to pleasure yet always be weary of our own monotony.

It is the onward movement in life that gives the meaning. Not where we are but whither we go decrees our habitation. The world is a thicket of pain and confusion until we *know* we are growing! Then the world is an avenue to Paradise. Nothing explains us to ourselves but the realization of our own advance; the consciousness of thinking, feeling, and wanting more, of having and giving more, of seeing, doing, and being more, of loving, striving, suffering, praying, and trusting more.

Life is either growth or death; life has no existence in itself. And the strange thing about life is that we do not see this. Why are children happy? Because they are *growing on all sides*. Why are men perplexed and women downhearted? Because they have ceased growing and commenced dying long before their time. At middle-age the body starts to disintegrate; but the rest of the man, the heart, mind, and soul, should then be only just prepared for real development. The secret of eternal youth? Eternal growth! Conquer the slow death of the physical by the rapid growth of the mental, psychic, emotional, spiritual, transcendental.

Growth is a bigger thing than we take it for. It is the motive, impulse, plan, and effect of the Universe. Death is the mortal, growth is the divine. And there could be no more stupendous error than to imagine, as the majority do, that *only children grow*. The record for growth in any family should be held by the grandparents. That is, unless there are great-grandparents.

Every kind of unfoldment, except the mere physical, belongs to maturity. Yet, strange to say, only the children watch themselves grow. When you were little, didn't you have a chimney corner, or the side of a door, where you proudly stood up as the months went by, and marked the highest point even with your stature? Maybe, too, you cheated; maybe you brushed your hair pompadour, maybe you stood on tiptoe, maybe you held the yardstick slanting — not to be dishonest, but to help yourself believe you had grown all that you possibly could!

Every child, young or old, needs a calendar, a yardstick, and a chimney corner. Yes, and a friend who can stand away a little, to see that the measure is honestly taken. The service incomparable of true friendship is to whisper our shortcomings so lovingly that we hear but the yearning to see in us perfection. Friendship is only unswerving devotion to a common ideal.

Sane Progress; what is it?

Many, many things; the first of which may perhaps be the possession of a right standard whereby to judge ourselves. There are few of us who are not self-deceived, largely because we spend all our time watching our neighbors. Moreover, we find self-examination irksome and fatal to our pride. Hence, whatever growth we achieve comes not through emulation of ourselves but through competition with our adversaries. A motive and a method absolutely wrong.

Example of this: Who is the college hero, adored, flattered and idolized out of all semblance to his natural worth? The gridiron warrior, beefy and sinewy, shaggy and crude, born that way and getting more so all the time. What virtue that an ox remain an ox? The athlete grows not by heaving huge weights or sprinting for a medal, but by tensing the muscles of his mind and striving to expand his sympathies. Why the Field Day prizes to burly John Fisticuff, who already has more body than he needs?

The plight of the bookworm is ever more pathetic. Little Mister Meticulous Moses Megalocephalous, be-ribboned, be-spectacled, wearisome and wan, how shall he advance with due precision? Get a husky lad on either side of him, gently propel him to the margin of the river, then with cordial informality — chuck him in! The first religious duty of a bookworm is to learn to paddle for himself.

Institutions are made not for growth but for safety. That is why rewards proposed by institutions are usually meaningless — they elevate the obvious, while scorning the essential, which is always more subtle. In the race toward Heaven the prizes are for those who have seen and outrun their own hidden weaknesses.

The next factor in Sane Progress is a recognition of what really constitutes growth. A popular form of salutation is "How are you getting on?" Yet the man who gets on without getting in other directions will presently have a chance to get off and meditate. Once let a human being declare a limit for himself, saying, "I will go by this way and by no other" — then do fiends and angels unite to encompass his destruction. The lives of the great prove this: that if a man really wants to grow he will suddenly be whirled from his little pathway of human expectation and flung upon the wide thoroughfare of God's intention. If your plans all succeed, they were not God's plans. Nature is loveliest after the storm; so God is nearest after the ruin of mortal ambitions. A blinding grief, an overwhelming loss, a terrible privation, or a bitter punishment, is the universal gateway through which all souls pass into Freedom. The need of this is clear enough; the average human life is one long compromise, and when the veils are parted they must also be rent. Growth follows upheaval. Half human paroxysm, half divine peace, the measure of attainment is how we value a crisis. Lethargy should madden us — and riot give us poise.

The world is full of men and women who today are as they were twenty years ago, and forty years hence they will still be the same. Such people died before they were born. You can't be yourself and be the same to-morrow. Every day, every hour, may witness all the seasons of the year to the soul. And, very often, one flash of illumination has turned a cringing slave into a lord of cosmos. Why do most people *want* to live, feeling nothing, thinking nothing, wanting, loving, and hating nothing? Why don't they die if only for the interest of the thing? Life without growth has all the sting of death without the joy of resurrection. Is it any wonder that the majority fret and worry, being half dead, and blind to the fact? Nothing matters but growth. It is the only human necessity.

What then constitutes growth? Progress to the individual — and there is no other permanent kind — moves in five directions: *inward, upward, downward, outward, onward.* A knowledge of self, a hold on God, a belief in Nature, a sympathy with the world, and a clean, strong, dominant purpose, to govern all the rest; these together, and each growing, make Sane Progress.

Sane Progress first is *inward.* Even a little self-analysis betrays how many of our habits are inherited, borrowed, or induced with no understanding or volition on our part. Why do we eat three meals a day? Why do we choose woolen underwear and change the weight of it twice a year? Why do we ventilate our house — or neglect to — in a certain way? Why do we fear "catching cold"? Why do we accept public opinion as trustworthy, basing our action upon it? Why do we mold our politics, religion, and life-work after the pattern used and worn out by our forefathers? To most of us, the realm of our own nature is a wild, forbidden land. Yet all beneficent discovery proceeds from this. Who controls our "moods"? What are they anyhow? Have we a chronic ailment; do we ever fall ill? The fundamental blasphemy is sickness, and clergymen everywhere have begun to realize it. Are we expressing the huge possibilities born in every living soul; or do we feel like slaves and chattels? We can, if we will, be lords of our own world; and that world, as we occupy it, grows to fill the Universe.

Sane Progress next is *upward.* Do we feel at home amid the stars? If not, we are mere babes aimlessly creeping in a closed chamber, while beyond the door whose latch we cannot reach lies a very palace of rare, glistening beauty. Worlds are but anterooms to space. Cares — world cares — that hem us in and cloud our vision will all be swept away when we fling the portal of our consciousness wide, ever wider, to the sunlight of universal truth and the breath of God in the heavens. For the momentary work of a little human life we have taken human bodies and live among men. But our destiny immortal and our solace eternal lie beyond. A sense of personal infinity, all-impelling, all-revealing, must claim us for its own before we can do the big things we are here for.

Sane Progress next is *downward*. Not how beautifully we can dream, but how mightily we can grapple with the ugly thing at hand; this proves where we are. I suppose there is nothing more useless (I know there is nothing more exasperating) than a so-called student of esoterics who in the face of a serious problem or a mean, disagreeable job smiles in a bland, superior sort of way and musically murmurs a hypnotic shibboleth! Such illumination is mirage. Heaven must be seen beyond the world, but entered through the world. The people who despise earth haven't made its acquaintance. A mud bath is actually a spiritualizing process. Not by deserting our bodies, but by making them over, do we convey our souls. Muscle and nerve and sinew, flesh and brain and bone and blood, give to the soul its only fortress whence to wage its human battle.

Sane Progress next is *outward*. Having found ourselves, the needful thing for us is to lose ourselves. We must plunge into the midst of the fray, and by combat, not by meditation, liberate the powers of the soul. Knowledge alone measures responsibility. Truth to be kept must be shared. The plight of the world, the problem of the man next door, the sorrow of the stranger whom we pass on the highway, the longing or the heartache of our own kinsfolk — these call to us no less than the hunger for growth of our individuality. At some time in our lives we must yield all for another, else our lives, at the last, are meaningless.

Sane Progress next is *onward*. The men who grow most are the men with colossal ambitions. The price of material success is always a form of spiritual discipline. We make our moral backbone by riding rough shod over obstacles; and we never get the nerve to do this save as a huge ambition leads us on. There is a bliss of divine calm and there is a bliss of human triumph. Once we have tasted either, we must have the other.

Now for the application.

The world at large, and American in particular, during the past five years has witnessed a veritable epidemic of unusual thought. New sects, cults, modes of healing and schools of philosophy everywhere abound. Each is true and good up to a certain point, then each fails because the *progress of its devotees has become one-sided.*

There are people to whom their own stomach is the Universe. Naturally, having eaten, they "see stars," comets, nebulae, and approaching storms galore. They weigh each morsel of food with a gravity befitting the inaugural of solar systems. They have made Pepsin king, Calories queen, and Jeremiah Longface prime minister. Their disposition, in wild revolt, betrays the inner chaos, and a gloomy line of tedious, turbulent health reformers perpetrates itself on the world.

There are other people who are lodged amid the clouds. Nothing arouses them but the interstellar cycle of the soul through a million speculative lives. Hence they are interested in nothing on earth — and fit for nothing. May there not be such a thing as a transcendental Polly Pry? The study of occultism enlarges our vision, heightens our perception, broadens our sympathy, and empowers our faith; but the *worship* of occultism incapacitates us for a healthy, sane, joyous human life.

There are other people whose fetish is barbarism. They retire to the woods; taboo knives and forks, barbers, clean clothes, and civilized manners; take the animals for model citizens; and hilariously vegetate. They do this until they get arrested; then they are metamorphosed into anarchists or political reformers. And the world goes on just the same.

There are other people in whom the fever of social unrest burns brightly. They organize, agitate, and labor — earnestly enough but sadly mistaken. The world grows better as the man grows greater; it is the man, not the community, whose growth signifies. Worlds are but playgrounds for individuals.

There are other people to whom life is merely a struggle for wealth, fame, position, or perhaps the adulation of a host of followers. They are "concentrating" on a goal of achievement, and relaxing their grip on themselves. With an altruistic motive, they could be messiahs. Lacking that, they are conscious failures in spite of their worldly pinnacle. The saddest, most hopeless failure is the successful man who has acquired *things* before he mastered *principles*.

The aim of all development must be symmetry. Whether growing inward, upward, downward, outward, or onward, we will reach perfection sooner by taking a different route from the one we have traveled.

Sane Progress may be told in three words: *Bravery, Breadth, Brotherhood.*

It is no easy thing to leave the multitude in search of Truth. It is a much harder thing, having made friends with Truth, to remain loyal. Not as a fad, or a pride, or a passing whim of curiosity, but as a quest eternal and crusade indomitable must the endeavor be to know and have and live truly.

Then to belief must come balance. Every soul follows its own predestined path. Ours is best for us — our neighbor's best for him. Interference would retard both.

Yet, we can shine without interfering. And a loving sympathy, wide as the heavens, clear as the sun, is perhaps the ultimate signal of progress.

CHAPTER 16

Ways of Reading Character

A THEORY, to be effective, must be yoked with its opposite. Because a theory, like a mustang, runs wild until harnessed and put to work.

An untamed theory is flighty as a bucking broncho; until we can drive our theories instead of being driven by them, we are in no safe condition. Beware the man with a loose theory, charging head-long, seeking whom it may devour. For such a theory is a dangerous animal — whether called Socialism, Vegetarianism, Anti-vaccination or New Thought.

I actually know people who cannot eat their dinner unless they have brought in their pocket a shaggy slab of dyspepticated bread, to munch between courses; there are others who cannot sleep soundly without having auto-suggestionized themselves into psychic rapport with self-imagined ghosts; still others, set upon by a momentary pain, telegraph their mental "healer" to save them from their doom by a species of twentieth-century incantation called a "vibratory treatment." Such folks are riding a mustang theory. You can't help them, for they can't let go. But keep out of their way.

The man who is radical in belief should be conservative in action; the man who responds to music and art should force himself under routine; the man whose business makes him hard should be twice as loving in his family; the man whose temptation is to entertain gloom should memorize ifunny yarns, and write optimistic essays for the psychological magazines. Thus, the mild good in each human tendency would be retained, while the extreme bad in a tendency untethered would be avoided.

This principle should be noted, in the current epidemic of Optimism. Many adherents of Higher Thought claim that every man is potentially, essentially, perfect. Therefore they treat him as perfect. Therefore they wax grievously disappointed — when he borrows their last dollar, decamps with their reputation, or runs off with their wife.

Every man *should* be trusted — trusted and watched! Lack of shrewdness does not mean excess of spirituality, it means intellectual laziness and moral blindness. Cutting your eye-teeth is no sign of retrogression. A baby-smile is a lovely thing to see; but if you can't wear a baby-smile on a man's head, you'd better leave off the smile.

Would you win material success? *Study people.* Learn to profit by their mistakes, to strengthen yourself through their weakness, to satisfy their wants and get paid for doing it, to lead their ambitions and supply their rewards, to hold in your hand their mainspring of motive and hasten or hinder their action as you will. Not wrongfully, not even selfishly; but that destiny may be shaped by the man who *knows*.

He who attains knows himself; he who achieves knows his neighbors. The most cold-blooded financial proposition resolves into playing on the warmest human affections and the subtlest human desires. Men differ in how they work because they differ in why they work. We have heard much, recently, of "Scientific Management," that wonderful combination of anatomy, psychology and economics which enables a man to double or treble his daily output of work, yet be less tired after earning more. Every man who toils should study this — whether he be a college dean or a bricklayer. Yet the system rightfully begins with the *choice* of men for the business or profession they are to enter. Every man is born with a certain knack. Fit your work to your knack, then your work succeeds and you are happy; try to do another man's work with a knack that isn't yours, then your work fails and you are miserable. Every employee should be selected by a scientific reader of character, and placed in that department where his talents will make him most proficient. Psychology is the most practical study in the world; but its value will not be recognized until psychologists put away their mortar-boards and break into business.

Go to the opposite extreme — that of sentiment. What makes marriages unhappy? Selfignorance, and the growing incompatibility based upon it. Courtship is a kind of moral polish, with which young folks whitewash themselves so that their faults may not appear to each other. Oftener than not, a fleeting whim governs the selection of a life-mate. The honeymoon is crucial because it spells candor — the woman's false hair and the man's false courtesy both meet the discard where false things end. There should be a twofold pre-nuptial test, whereby *knowledge* and *sincerity* are guaranteed — knowledge for one's self and sincerity for the other. In their physical, emotional, mental and spiritual make-up, two people are designed for each other, or they are not. Who knows? Who even tries to know? There should be a legal standard of conditions and requirements covering these four planes, with a table of minimum percentages in the hands of every clergyman or magistrate who officiates at weddings, and a fine imposed for each failure to compute the couple's fitness by the table. Then Susie would know if John was a brute, and John would know if Susie was a gad-about, and each would be spared the sorrow of disillusionment.

How do we judge our neighbors, whom we think we know? How do we distinguish friends, foes and strangers, from each other? How do we choose our companions, engage our employees, determine the playmates for our children? Ten to one by some artificial standard of measurement which conveys not the real man but the social shell in which he moves. Among these artificial standards are those of wealth, aristocracy, culture, education, popularity, family history, nationality, morality and religion; — all of which may be inherited, bought or begged; none of which portrays the individual concealed beneath appearances. Hence the countless misunderstandings that cause the heartache in the world.

How read a man's character wisely and justly? By the man himself; not by the family he came from, or by the clothes he wears, or by the tongue he speaks, or by the place he occupies. Every feature, curve and line in the human body means something. It did not happen so. It was produced mentally before shaped physically. It was prefigured in the subtle body. It is a plain result of a plain cause — to those who have insight.

CHAPTER 17

Man and His Community

A GROWN man is ten men.

He is, of course, a leader in his business or profession. He is, moreover, nine additional men; a householder, a provider, a husband, a father, a neighbor, a mystic, a warrior, a statesman, a humanitarian.

Each of these nine men I would call a "plusman" — he is plus the ordinary man in respect to wisdom, power, character. And I would define the "superman" as the embodiment of these nine plusmen in a single individual. The measure of a man is not his height or his weight, but his reply to this question: "How many kinds of plusman am I — how far have I yet to go to reach the superman stage?"

The curse of civilization is the preponderance of half-grown men. We see them everywhere — in commerce, education, law, medicine, politics, religion. The half-grown man is content to succeed in his job — and fail everywhere else. It takes a big man to focus on his job — but a bigger man to forget it! And the biggest man of all smiles at himself for needing a job — he ought to be independently rich, and able to spend his time profitably, in science or invention or music or philosophy or reform.

This eternal straining for industrial efficiency grows to be weariness to the flesh, and vexation to the spirit. The ant hurries and scurries hither and yon, bent on nothing but lugging a load of food to a spot of safety. Herein is the ant efficient, being only an ant. Herein is a man not efficient, being a man.

The aim and sum of efficiency is personality. A man should do better work to make him a bigger man. The most efficient business man is only 10 per cent, efficient while he neglects the other nine men he ought to be. Efficiency study is primarily self-interest, being scientifically based on the first law of nature, which is self-preservation. But efficiency study is ultimately social service, being ethically based on a higher law, which is the Golden Rule.

I have seen a professional man raise his earning capacity 5,000 per cent, by means of the principles and methods we advocate. I have seen a corporation president create a demand for the product of his company ten times greater than the company could fill. I have seen a school principal attract about 100,000 students for a branch of study never taught until he taught it. I have seen many a man, trained in Efficiency, perform deeds that would in the olden days have been called miracles. But I do not consider one of these men efficient as a man, merely because he is efficient as a cog in a business wheel.

A thoroughly evolved, highly organized man is a compound of physical, emotional, intellectual and spiritual forces, the relative importance of which we would designate thus: physical, 10 per cent; intellectual, 20 per cent.; emotional, 30 per cent; spiritual, 40 per cent. In your business your personal development is mostly confined to the physical and intellectual 30 per cent of you — what are you doing with the remaining 70 per cent, of you? When a man's brain is defective or deficient, we call him an idiot or a lunatic, we are sorry for him, we drag him to an asylum and bravely lock him up. The average man — the "successful" business man — is apt to be an *emotional* idiot and a *spiritual* lunatic; he has about the same knowledge of, and command over, his feelings, desires and aspirations as a person "out of his mind" has in respect to the functions of cerebration. Not your brain, but your solar plexus, is the galvanic battery to make you a worldpower! Not what you think but what you feel drives you to your goal; what you think merely paves the road, but what you feel moves you on and up, ever on and up — road or no road!

Have you learned how to *feel* efficiently? No matter what you say, I say you haven't. Because if you had, you would be such a colossal worldfigure that you wouldn't take time to read my articles. Would Napoleon or Lincoln ask me, or anybody else, how to become efficient? I should hope not. The man whose heart beats high enough and fast enough has no need of a standard or a clock — he makes his own. The height of your dream and the depth of your resolve — these measure you. And these are of the heart, not of the brain.

Every ambitious man should learn to be efficient in his home and community, not merely for the sake of the home and community, but even more for his own sake. Not otherwise can he ever unlock the emotional and spiritual energies in him and extend his ego fully, even through the realm of commerce. A man never reaches the height of business success until he gains the elevation of utter absorption in something outside of business. The needs of his home, or of his community, or of both, should be to a good business man the real reason for learning how to meet the needs of his business.

Each of the nine plusmen that every man should be deserves a paragraph of question and suggestion. Each demands vocational training that our colleges ought to give, but do not.

THE EFFICIENT HOUSEHOLDER

When you go home at night, are you a social integer — or a social cipher? A woman never respects any kind of masculine cipher, and you have lost home influence just to the degree that you have failed to give your wife sympathetic help in solving her many household problems. Your home knowledge must equal her business knowledge, if the domestic partnership works out properly. Why expect her to be a graduate in marketing and accounting methods, when you are a primary scholar in home decoration and feminine psychology? When your wife has trouble with the help, as of course she has, what do you do about it? Scold rashly? Or bluster vainly? Or just slink away, on the pretext of having a headache or a sudden weariness? You are supposed, being a man of affairs, to know how to manage employees. Your wife is not. Why don't you teach her? You get a vacation every week from Saturday afternoon 'till Monday morning — or 52 vacations a year, plus your annual holiday. How many periods of absolute rest does your wife take in a year? Remember that, if she is a good housekeeper, she cannot rest at home — she must get out and away. She wants moreover, an eight-hour workday as much as you do; why don't you, being a master of planning, show her how to plan for it? When she needs a new labor-saving device in the kitchen, do you buy it as cheerfully as you would install such a contrivance in your own office? These are but a few sample queries — you might well devote an evening to asking and answering forty or fifty more questions along the same line.

THE EFFICIENT PROVIDER

By this I mean literally the man who "sees ahead" for his family — not merely pays their bills. No one born with a "gold spoon in his mouth" ever learned to eat with it. Your job as head of a family is not so much to give your folks money as to teach them how to earn it, save it, and spend it, equally well. Has each member of your family a personal bank account? Does each live on the budget plan, successfully? Could each dine at Sherry's or the Waldorf with grace and elegance and $5 each for the meal — or dine cheerfully and thankfully off a piece of bread-and-butter and a dish of prunes in the kitchen? Do you carry both life and fire insurance, reliable and ample? Is your will drawn up, so as to be just and generous, and clear and complete? Have you made it unbreakable by any device of a lawyer? (I always enjoy telling a man to do something entirely impossible — then if he doesn't do it, I can always lay at his door any trouble that comes from taking my advice.) Do you keep all your valuable papers in a safe deposit vault or a fireproof home safe — and is each member of your household following your example? Could every person in your family over twelve years of age earn his or her own living if necessary? Do your folks all *enjoy* economizing? After such a question as the last I pause — the day of miracles is past! I judge the supreme test of a man as a provider would be that he induced his family to save money as cheerfully and persistently as they spend it. Why not? Should not building the future be as pleasant an occupation as wasting the present?

THE EFFICIENT HUSBAND

Good wives are born — good husbands must be made, or rather must make themselves. Wife-instincts are normal, husband-instincts are supernormal. Through ages women have been wives perforce. They have thus learned how — we say by "intuition." Men have *not* learned how to be husbands; they have not learned how to be emotional wizards and moral giants. To be an efficient husband, you must have the shrewdness of all the demons in the universe, and the goodness of all the angels, thoroughly and sweetly combined. How? Am I then a Solomon, that ye should ask me this thing? The first duty of a husband is to learn to be a Galahad and a Bluebeard, both in the same breath! You must be everything — and its opposite. Else your wife cannot be a happy, wholesome and useful woman. She expects you to need her — and lead her; to want her — and worship her; to pet her — and dominate her; to soothe her — and hurt her; to protect her — and liberate her; to idolize her — and teach her; to pamper her — and empower her; to hide her far away — and show the whole world your pride in her. A full-grown man can do all this; but he is scarce. Fineness and force, perfectly united, a normal woman asks of her husband — or would ask it if she dared believe in him that much. A faded love-letter with the breath of roses still upon it means more to a woman than a marble palace with the sentiment gone. But you must give her a palace, too! Else were she not a woman. Perhaps, being stupid like most men, you ask me to be "practical." All right — what are you doing to help your wife carve her own career, independent of you? Unless you are a cave-man, you are a wifehelper, not just a wife-owner. What have you done to prove it? Are you making her destiny as vital to you as you expect yours to be to her? Do you know how many secret longings she has in her heart, that she never shared with you? It might be well to find out.

THE EFFICIENT FATHER

It takes a brave man to look his children in the face. Some of the bravest men I know can't do it. Most men don't even try to do it — they leave the job exclusively to their wives. Noble exhibition of manly strength! Do you see that all your children's questions are answered properly? Do you make each one feel that, next to his mother, you are his best friend in the world? Have you engaged in a special study of the opportunities and responsibilities involved in scientific fatherhood? When your children have to be disciplined, do you whip them — or scold them — or let them go unpunished — or leave the whole affair to mother? All bad methods. Are you merely a check-book and a check-rein by turns, drawing on each to make up for the way you draw on the other? There are masculine views and virtues needed in the training of both boys and girls that a mother, even the best mother, cannot supply. What are they? How many of them do you contribute to the necessary physical, mental and moral equipment of your children? The duty of the father, more than the mother, is to provide for the little folks their athletic and industrial training, financial competence, vocational guidance, personal system, social selection, knowledge of state-craft and world-events, moral backbone, spiritual nerve and sinew. As a father, are you a success?

THE EFFICIENT NEIGHBOR

I do not refer to the cheerfulness and alacrity with which you lend your lawn-mower, though I might do so to advantage. I refer to the knowledge you have of your neighbors' needs, and the effort you make to supply them. In every family there are problems that the family next door could help solve; yet the two families remain strangers. We have learned to exchange everything but experience; it is time we learned to exchange that — the most valuable, as the most costly, human possession. When we give a "party," we always invite the other idiots in our "set," and gage the affair by the amount of cake and punch the guests consume — while a beggar on the next street may be searching in vain for a crust of bread. We send millions overseas — not even knowing that in our own town are cases just as pitiful, of sorrow and destitution. Can't we find some way to be a little more neighborly — share a little with those who need so much?

[167]

THE EFFICIENT MYSTIC

A mystic is a man who draws his greatest power from Nature and from God. Every world-leader is a mystic. We may call his power magnetism, or enthusiasm, or energy, or will, or faith — no matter, it came from Nature and God. This all-conquering fire and force may be largely increased by music, art, poetry, philosophy, and other spare-time aids that unlock the subjective mind. Now the home and community need from the progressive man just the exercise of these forces whose results will, at the same time, expand him. Conquest merely crowns conviction. Power is the measure of purpose. The master of action was first master of inspiration; and the cry from the homes of the world has always been for the *man* who is inspired! He understands.

THE EFFICIENT WARRIOR

The ghastly but superb siege of Verdun was a miracle of human valor. Yet the brave who there fought and fell were blind — all blind. They fought to kill, instead of to *create*. The battles of to-morrow will be battles of construction — not of destruction. America needs a great army of knights of industry, knights of purity, knights of science, knights of peace. In your home town you can find intrenchments of evil as hard to take as was the fortress of Verdun. There is graft, corruption, child labor, disease, intemperance, poverty, profanity, gossip, slander, sex blasphemy and abuse. There is a modern need for a holy war. The newspapers tell us that 2,000,000 clubwomen are combining to reform the indecencies of the present styles in woman's dress. Can you picture 2,000,000 clubwomen combining to outlaw the cocktail, banish the cigaret, or elevate musical comedy? Why not? Should not the vices of men be fought by men as powerfully and bravely as the weaknesses of women are fought by women? A real man loves a good fight — and a man is not real till he gets in a good fight. What should you be fighting for — and against, in your community?

THE EFFICIENT STATESMAN

Inefficiency is the slogan of politicians — they feed and grow fat on it. The spoils system; lobby legislation; machine-made ballots and votes; political rotation in office; the self-advertising and electioneering of party candidates; these are but a few of the wastes and follies in our boasted democracy. The man who always "votes straight" always votes crooked. He mentally squints, or morally dodges. There is no efficient political party. The first one, if there ever is one, will be organized as a protest against all parties, and a union of the good in all parties. Meanwhile, if you are a Democrat, a Republican, a Socialist, a Prohibitionist, or an Anarchist, you might be discovering how some other party is better than yours, and thus be preparing to vote efficiently when, the day just before the millennium, an efficient party, on an efficient platform, adduces efficient argument for efficient support.

THE EFFICIENT HUMANITARIAN

A good business man is good to himself last. He is big enough and wise enough to make the Golden Rule one of his chief business regulations. The new type of successful man is both hardheaded and soft-hearted. He makes of his profit a protectorate. A famous organizer and economist says that "the leaders in the world fifteen years from now will be the men with the greatest power of social cooperation." This is already coming to be true. The heads of the great factories, mills and stores are devoting each year vast sums to purely social work among their employees — to hygienic and industrial education, home economics, music and art, athletics and recreation, personal welfare, moral supervision. The real profits in a business are the benefits to the community. When every business man has sense enough to learn this, he will double his profits and halve his troubles at the same time.

Now if, being a level-headed and large-hearted man, you should ask what you can do practically for your neighbors and community, we would answer, briefly and partially, as follows:

Investigate the national civic improvement societies. Get their literature, think it over, hand it around. Join one or more of these organizations; if possible found a branch in your locality. Look up the various efficiency movements, magazines, books, leaders, clubs and associations in the United States.

Obtain from the Efficiency Publishing Company, Woolworth Building, New York City, a clearing house for Efficiency literature, a list of titles of Efficiency books.

Apply to the nearest librarian for a list of the new books on social service and community betterment. Read one or two of these in your home circle, then adapt to the needs of your neighborhood. In this connection, study the recent developments of city government; such as the commission-manager plan, which has been tried in several hundred American cities, and proved successful, we understand, in over ninety per cent, of these places.

Learn what is being done, what further should be done, by your associated charities organization, by your local Board of Health, by your societies for temperance, industrial cooperation, social hygiene and moral education. Give your support wherever you can. Give time, thought, influence, money.

Get in touch with the remarkable advance now being made in Sunday school efficiency and church practicality. Many a business man should go to a modern Sunday school to learn how to organize his business. I have before me the community program of one of the leading religious denominations. This aims to cover prison reform; needs of rural communities, the home and the child; problems of industry and immigration; temperance and social hygiene; education for social service; national security and international peace. Your church may help you to solve the problems of your business. Learn how. Keep informed on the social work of your national church organization. Identify yourself with it, promote it all you can.

General Goethals declares that the most successful engineer of the future will be the man who knows the human side of engineering work, the man who is master of human construction. A final test of a great man is that he holds his great work to be man-building, not business-building. Make your business the finest in the world; but that your community may be better, and your home best of all.

THE EFFICIENT MAN'S TEST

FOR DETERMINING THE MENTAL AND MORAL SIZE OF A MAN IN HIS
HOME AND COMMUNITY

DIRECTIONS. Where answer is Yes, write numeral 5 in blank space opposite. Where answer is No, leave space blank. Where answer is partly affirmative, write numeral less than 5 denoting degree of assurance. For your percentage in home and community efficiency, add column of numerals. This Test is not complete, but may be held reliable so far as it goes.

1. Do your neighbors call you public-spirited, generous, philanthropic? _____

2. Are you trained in the masculine side of home efficiency? _____

3. Have you applied business methods to the organization of your household? _____

4. Do you help your wife to solve her home and parenthood problems? _____

5. Have you taught your wife and children the science of finance? _____

6. Has each member of your family a bank account, either checking or saving? _____

7. Do you carry ample insurance — fire, accident, and life? _____

8. Is your wife happier than just before she married you? _____

9. Have you made a scientific study of paternal duties and responsibilities? _____

10. Are you a friend, thoughtful and helpful, to all your neighbors? _____

11. Can you in your sphere of influence wield
    the subjective powers of the mind? _____

12. Are you a leading fighter in some good
    cause (preferably unpopular)? _____

13. Do you always vote for the best man,
    without regard to politics? _____

14. Have you investigated the new
    methods of municipal government
    and improvement? _____

15. Are you a member of a national, and a
    local, civic association? _____

16. Do you know that your public schools
    are under efficient teachers and
    modern methods? _____

17. Have you read and followed a standard
    book on social service? _____

18. Is your church doing scientific and
    effective community work? _____

19. Are you helping to carry out a modern
    charity program for the poor? _____

20. Do you want greater success in order to
    achieve greater usefulness? _____

    _____

Add column of numerals to find your approximate grade in home and community efficiency.

CHAPTER 18

The Fine Art of Giving

WE are grown to the extent that *giving* is our great purpose in life. The animal seeks — the angel bestows. And the man most divine is he who feels impelled to share, with his loved ones or the world, all that he has or is or hopes to be.

The flower in bud absorbs from the earth whatever it needs for growth; the flower in bloom returns, to the senses of all who pass that way, a beauty and a sweetness which the earth did not possess. Young *souls* reach out for elements to build their stature; old souls radiate the sweetness, love, and light that they have learned to draw from experience. Our age, in the cycle of the spheres, may be known by whether we grasp or whether we give with more power and exultation.

The poet who starves that his muse may be nourished; the martyr who dies that his faith may be sustained; the mother who not only braves death but braves it with a smile, that her dear ones may not see how she suffers for their sake — these know the quivering, poignant, sense of living through and through. For these give themselves, and nothing less is life to the Infinite Giver.

There is a bliss in sacrifice of which those have never dreamed who always save themselves. To give and give and give, with such abandon that all thought of self is burned away in the altar-fires of pure devotion; this translates the giver into Heaven while his body yet remains on the earth. Soul is fully satisfied only when body, heart and mind have been altogether spent, used, emptied, sacrificed, in rendering glorified service to the friend, or the work, most beloved. Do you suffer? Pour yourself out for another, lose yourself in the love of the other; when the self-obliteration is complete God will take possession of you and fill you with the joy of a new self divine. For this is the law of life; that the creator of what is immortal should be willing to die for his creation. Hardship? Not to the creator — only to the blind friends of the creator.

Contemplation of a great work of art brings to most of us a combined feeling of admiration and discontent. We delight in the charm of a lovely painting, the grace of a noble statue, the spell of a lilting melody, the lure of a haunting poem. Yet, underneath, we chafe at the commonness of our own lives, we long for a crimson thread of genius running through the dull gray web of earth's monotony.

Let us stop and think, however, what makes genius. Is it not, first of all, the willingness — the determination — the impulsion, to give to the world the best that is in a man? Why envy the artist? Our best may exceed his best — *when our willingness exceeds his willingness*. And the quickest way to find our best is to cultivate the spirit of giving.

Painting, sculpture, music, poetry, most of the fine arts, demand a certain kind of genius in the artist. But the essence of them all is the joy of self-surrender to a greater thing than self; and the fine art of giving, the finest in the world, may become to us all the channel for a new, divine expression. Sleeping poets, musicians, orators and evangels lie undiscovered in many human hearts, needing generosity and sympathy to burst the walls of stone that surround those who live just for self. Only the love-light shows how great we are; only the friendship-glow reveals to us our best.

The artist works for love — the artisan for money. So may our common toil be changed into sublime creation, as we learn to labor with loving hands and hearts. He who gives more than he is paid for giving finds himself paid twice over; first by a crowning sense of freedom, of owing no man anything; then by a strange new vigor of self-respect and self-determination, stirring him to achieve his utmost regardless of the world's estimate told in the world's pay. Giving more and better service is the clue to "getting on."

But the fine art of giving demands caution no less than devotion. The born giver needs wisdom as much as the born saver needs generosity. The true gift not only embodies him who gives, but establishes him who receives, in a sweetness, breadth and strength before unrealized. How many people, after a Christmas celebration or a wedding ceremony, are as *free* as they were before? Gifts to be genuine must be spontaneous — a glance at the calendar makes them commercial. For he who gives from a sense of duty but pays his conscience hush-money on account of his lack of courage. Most wedding-invitations are barefaced tolls on friendship. Marriage gifts should represent personal ideals. Send your friend a book of poems, a folio of music, a symbolic painting or a rare bit of sculpture, for the nuptial token — something where the meaning outweighs the form. Cupid's arch foe is cupidity.

Any form of giving becomes a fine art when liberality and discretion, loyalty and justice, affection and aloofness, are equally blended. And not the size of a gift, but the appropriateness, determines the value. Hence we can all be philanthropists, for we all have something helpful to share with those in need.

Giving *money* is a fine art.

The gift that represents money is oftener incubus than inspiration — have you never witnessed the sad plight of those in possession of things they dared not give away, didn't like to throw away, couldn't possibly use, and hadn't room to house? An ounce of thoughtfulness in a gift is worth more than a pound of gold. The real token of affection does not obligate the recipient in any way, except to enjoy the gift and love the giver more. There is a woman who keeps a list of the Christmas presents received this year, with the probable value tagged on each in order that next year she buy for the donor a trinket of equal money-weight! Few go to this extreme commercialism, but many feel indebted to a degree that mars the interchange of pure good-will. Honest friends want just to be remembered, with a smile or tear and a prayer. So, because we are all growing to be more honest, we now send many beautiful cards of remembrance at Easter and Christmas, where before we sent costly gifts to a chosen few. The kindest beneficence is to scatter sunshine through the world. And this costs nothing but to live the radiant life.

Giving *sympathy* is a fine art.

There is probably more energy lost in waste emotion than through any other channel. Observe the wayward children spoiled by excessive kindness; the criminals in prison-cells loaded with flowers bought by foolish, neurotic women; the indolent wives and the brutal husbands, needing a guiding hand of iron more than velvet; the cynics, mourners, and pessimists in whom the feeling has either frozen, or been drained, or turned bitter. The majority of those who suffer need spunk more than sympathy. They have erred and they must pay. They are invalids and want drastic treatment to make them well. Watch how a trained nurse handles a complainer. She listens to his murmur, she responds to his wail, but she gives him what he should have for recovery — not what he would have for ease. And if surgery is indicated, she stands ready with the probe. We all need trained nurses for the heart, mind, and soul of us — cool, brave, incisive operators who will probe for the cause of our grief, poverty, oppression or disaster, and who though sympathizing with our pain will cut the offense clean out of us. To sympathize really with a friend, we must first see through and beyond him, to what he will be with his weakness gone. For weakness is the winding corridor to woe.

Giving *time* is a fine art.

As a time-saver, the business man is a model (and only the time-saver is of any worth as a timegiver). Try to reach the president of a big corporation, and you begin to learn the value of minutes. The utmost audience he grants you is momentary, and your wits must work like chainlightning to save you from the corresponding flash of his eye. Women callers should take a course of business training if only to teach them how to say good-by this side of sundown. If any man could buy the time consumed in babble, he would be the money-king of the world. He who spends himself in speech has least to show of any profligate. Learn how to send your friends home when they ought to go; if they won't listen gladly they aren't your friends; and if you can't tell them easily you aren't their friend. Efficiency is but complete use of one's time and talent; employ your time, and your talent will develop itself. Time should be given for no reason but to help or be helped. This test would annul most of our social obligations.

Giving *opportunity* is a fine art.

Do you know where, in your town, a starving, homeless man may find relief? Here in New York we have the Salvation Army, the Volunteers of America, the St. Andrew One Cent Coffee Stands, the famous "Bread Line," numerous cheap hotels and practical mission houses, where for little or nothing a friendless pauper may subsist long enough to get a new start. Carry this same principle higher, and you find struggling artists, poets, musicians, scientists, inventors; young people founding a home on a pittance; misfits in all the walks of life; strangers in the city — and in the country neighbors often called by name yet little known — pining for companionship; mental, emotional and spiritual paupers too proud to beg yet needing the resource of a charitable institution. The time will come when all charity will consist in putting a man in line with opportunity. Need must be matched with knowledge — knowledge of one's power and of the place to use it. We should treat beggars as we treat babies — confine them until we have them educated. Some day our prisons will be only mutual improvement societies, and every jail will have a waiting-list of positions ready for those who learn command of themselves while in custody.

Giving *service* is a fine art.

Service may be the most dignified thing in the world. The house-maid who is slatternly, the office worker who skimps hours, the ditch-digger who grumbles and holds himself a menial, these find service distasteful because they have not put themselves into what they are doing. They are chafed by the ragged edges of their own divided personality. Put your head and your heart into the work of your hands — then watch drudgery leap into joy. Every public or private servant needs two things; a scientific training, and a sympathetic motive. This truth fits equally politicians and coach-men. Lacking science they bungle their work; lacking sympathy they abuse their trust. The ultimate value of service may be gaged by this question: Does it add to the self-respect of both master and servant?

Giving *truth* is a fine art.

The great hurt common to all earnest men and women is voiced in the cry that comes to us so often — "If I could only make others see truth as I see it!" But you do not want them to, their truth must be the truth they can live, and they cannot live your truth. Pray for the wisdom and power to live your truth; that will make them want to see and live theirs. With some bodies some foods never agree; with some souls some truths never agree. If your neighbor's truth satisfies him, God feeds him; if it does not, he will judge the wholesomeness of your truth by your mental soundness and spiritual attractiveness. One-sided occult teaching, biased health advice, premature sex instruction and reform; these examples of partial or misplaced truths are wofully in evidence all about us. Distrust the man who calls himself any one thing; for the many things that he is not make the one thing that he is trivial by comparison.

Giving *love* is a fine art.

Ask any wife and mother. She will not answer in words; but if you look in her eyes when you speak her husband's name, you will know whether he is a dreaming, deft artist — or whether he himself was born of clay. Yet the ideals of men are nobler than the ideals of women; would that men were strong enough to hold themselves to the standards they create for their wives! Only as love for an ideal is merged in love for a personality can the human love endure. The children and parents, the brothers and sisters, the husbands and wives who grow apart have only missed the oneness of the human and divine. "Breach of promise" suits? Impossible, absurd, pitiful. Breach of purpose, breach of purity, breach of power, but not breach of promise. True love promises nothing yet performs all. The only guarantee that a lover asks is to be allowed to love, more and better. From the cradle to the grave, we are finding ourselves just as we are learning our need and capacity for love. For as we love, we create; and as we create, we are like God. Would you die for some one? Can you live for some one? Do you belong to some one — every inch and atom of you, every hope and thrill and longing, every joy and every sorrow, every little human thing and every great sublime thing of the eternal spaces? Only as you can answer yes with all your soul are you taught in the language of Heaven. For the speech of angels is devotion, and the alphabet of God is sacrifice.

V. FREEDOM

CHAPTER 19

Freedom the Goal of Life

THE finished man is free.

And the fact that we are all slaves proves how young we are in the evolution of the world.

I have never seen a man who was free. Every man is bound to some possession, some person, some habit, custom or tendency, some fear, weakness or desire. And the godlike possibilities of the human soul remain as limp and futile as the wings of a great -bird cruelly imprisoned in a cage whose iron bars are gilded to deceive. The first mark of the slave is to gloss over his limitations. And we all do that — instead of meeting them squarely and breaking their ugly hold.

You cannot restrict the body of a child without incurring protest from the child. If you were such a monster as to put a helpless baby into chains the law would compel you to desist. But what of your own mind? That is more delicate, more fragile, more precious, than even the soft, rosy form of a babe. And if you could have a picture of your mind, you would see a fettered, maimed, distorted thing robbed of its wonderful powers by the superstitions, conventions, halftruths and compromises that subtly enmesh and strangle it. We should all be geniuses if we had thought for ourselves, and our parents for themselves.

I love the true iconoclast. He may be rash, unwise, premature, but he is at least independent. And all the immortal works of man have been wrought in a spirit of freedom.

If you have never been thought "peculiar," you may know you are commonplace; for the individual is always peculiar. And if you stop to care what people think, you are blinded by the dust of dalliance, you are out of step with progress. The onlookers at life do the clamoring — the soldiers have no time for anything but fighting.

What is freedom?

Not fanaticism, not protest, not idleness, not arrogance, not despotism, not any of the things urged by the anarchist, who of all men is enslaved by his own obsession.

Freedom is the conscious power to express any, all, or none of yourself when you will, as you will, because you will. This, you observe, is the opposite of license. Freedom means expansion, expansion means exercise, exercise means skill, skill means work — and how few of those who rant freedom are willing to work! Idleness, which is the boast of those who *talk* freedom, is really trespass on the time and temper of others.

Freedom, like money, is wasted on those who never earned it. Undirected freedom is vagrancy. Who is really free — the ragged tramp or the rich traveler? Freedom means equipment no less than expanse. It is foolish to long for opportunity without the power to meet it.

Freedom costs more than any other boon of life — that is why so few attain it.

Do you want to know the price of freedom? *Infinite patience.*

Watch Paderewski on the platform, and you murmur "How easily he plays!" Watch him in the long, weary hours of isolation when he grimly attacks one exercise three hundred times before he has it conquered; then you exclaim "How deathly hard he works!" Would you be free? Gather your chains more closely about you, for a greater speed in your handicap race. The winning athlete glories in the handicap. Fate sets a handicap for none but a winner.

By the long hard path of human struggle we may reach the sunny mount of freedom — and the most of us travel that road. But a shorter, smoother avenue winds along the calm retreat of divine meditation — and the few great souls of the world have experienced this. We do not lack the *power* to break our chains and cast them down forever; we lack the courage, the poise, the skill, the persistence. Nothing from without can bind us, no man ever could enslave us; we are judged by our own prejudice, convicted by our own weakness, shackled and imprisoned by our own ignorance. None is our master except as he is master of himself; and the chains that we carry, we have fitted to our own limitations. When we see this, we change protest into power.

Go to any jail and you find a sullen mob of prisoners, helpless in their manacles, chafing at restraint, ugly with impotence. Yet the bondage lies not in the bonds. For the man who calls himself "The Handcuff King" only smiles at the rivets and the locks of machine-made fetters; in any prison, he forms his own method of escape. From the mental confinement and spiritual gloom in which most men live, we can safely emerge when we have developed our own powers of self-emancipation.

Are you free?

Here is a question that will soon determine. Is there any one thing, any one person, any one condition of life, that you must have to make you happy? If so, you are a slave.

Might all your friends go, all your possessions vanish, all your hopes end in ruin, the world itself pass away — but you remain calm and steadfast? If not, you are only a chattel, bound to the whim of Fate. Would you experience a new kind of happiness? *Learn to do without whatever you think you need most.*

We know how a child cries when he can't have what he wants, or when his toys are taken from him. Yet how many of us have really outgrown the child-impatience and the child-rebellion? Because we lack a certain trivial, imaginary good, we make ourselves wretched with self-pity or selfdisparagement. Rather, should we voluntarily dispose of much that we now possess, for the danger in most possessions lies in their obscuring the realities. We see God not in the midst of grasping, but in the midst of letting go.

The only safe reason for wanting things is the expectation of giving them away. And not so much to be philanthropic as to be free. The typical charity worker gives rein to his own emotions, but curbs the advance of those he considers paupers. Giving men *things* makes men prisoners, giving men *truths* makes men lords.

What are the forces that enslave us?

Anything, everything, that blocks the way to our ideal. Have you a clear, definite, systematic, ideal of what you long to be and do? And how is your personality, your way of thinking, your mode of living, holding you back? Freedom to the great is not so much abandon as accomplishment. The resolute shaping of our own immediate life according to our own firm standard leads to the most gigantic liberation. We shall never be free to express ourselves until we have been free to command ourselves.

The highest type of freedom is not the merry child, or the indolent troubadour, or even the pale ascetic. It is the stern business man who has kept his finer sense of things in spite of the din of battle, and whose vision stays clear where the grime is thickest. Running away from ugly things only gives them a better chance to flourish. Make of your life a challenge to all that suggests compromise, then feel the joy of independence.

Around the human soul many films gather, day by day. Everything untrue leaves its mark upon us. Even what is less than true chills and thwarts our soul-powers. In how many lives is the whole truth operative? In none. Who but the martyrs have been honest with themselves? And what, beside this, is worthy of a moment's consideration? We are not free unless we would rather die than compromise.

From all outer impositions we must liberate ourselves, before we can approach the measure of our destiny. From the dominion of things; from the trespass of thoughts; from the goad of desire; from the wound of memory; from the treadmill of habit; from the blindfold of prejudice; from the spell of sensation; from the drain of emotion; from the chill of intellect; from the web of temperament; from the veil of personality; from the snare and pit of human pride; from all these hindering shapes and shadows we must be free.

The human soul is but a channel through which flows a divine stream of energy. The efficient man keeps the channel clear. And to do this, he must look upon the world merely as a field through which he passes, not as a marsh in which he settles. The buoyancy to rise above the murkiness of life, and remain untinged by the dark sediment of experience — this denotes a man filled and impelled by the Universal Spirit.

Freedom is the force to express the underlying good in every human trait, without the admixture of the superficial error. It is the purity of the saint blent with the power of the sinner, the fire of the zealot fused with the poise of the sage, the dream of the poet guiding the tool of the drudge, the song of the troubadour gaily rising over the sullen clang of the forge. Freedom is sanctity without solemnity, mirth without flippancy, toil without drudgery, play without folly, care without worry, system without slavery, abandon without vice, fervor without fanaticism, delicacy without frailty, strength without violence, courage without rashness, sweetness without insipidness, shrewdness without selfishness, love without blindness, devotion without narrowness, life without limitation. When will the first man among us be free?

CHAPTER 20

A Declaration of Freedom

To dream without apology;

To act without regret;

To have convictions that are unconquerable and inviolable;

To work with the might and the skill of a man — but play with the ardor, and sleep with the faith, of a little child;

To owe nothing, earn all, give much, and save a little;

To keep an ambition that girdles the globe — then to watch possessions vanish with a smile;

To value comradeship and cling to the arms of dear ones — but to regard solitude the true source of power;

To emulate heroes and exalt the world's pioneers — yet imitate no man nor hold any greater than oneself;

To throw the world away, in pursuit of a cherished ideal;

To live one's own belief with a quiet, dauntless courage — to respect every other man's belief;

To find the greatest joy in the simple things of life — but to move as a lord amid the huge things;

To master all that men call wisdom — then to be infinitely humble in the presence of the vast Unknown;

To revel in the sweetness and glory in the strength of the perfect human body — yet to care for the body only as revealing the soul;

To forget the past, and create a splendid future out of each honest day as it comes;

To be always contented with what one has — but ever unsatisfied with what one is;

To be calm in sorrow and brave in defeat — yet kind and gentle in the hour of triumph;

To serve, and to rule, with equal majesty;

To make happiness for oneself — then be happiest in sharing it;

To delight in the friendship of children;

To lift the burden of those oppressed — then teach them how to bear it with cheerfulness and poise;

To banish fear, even the fear of death, knowing that death but releases the soul for wider activity;

To see only good everywhere;

To know and be oneself;

To voice that within which cries for expression;

To love — and let go;

THIS IS TO BE FREE.

CHAPTER 21

"Thank You, Pain"

WHEN we suffer, this should be our first mark.

For Pain is the kindest friend we have — the only one whose presence always helps.

If a stranger, happening by in the dead of night and seeing our house afire, should suddenly forget his manners and rudely jerk the door-bell, rattle the shutters or even smash the window-pane in his anxiety to save us — would we hate him, or stop to abuse him for disturbing our slumbers? Exactly so with Pain. He may have forgotten his manners, but he comes with a message greater than manners. If he interrupts us, he does it with a purpose; the house of our body or mind is burning, and Pain rushes in to warn us of our danger while we sleep.

There was never a pang but the lack of it would have meant greater woe. When we understand this fully, we are glad to suffer as much and as long as need be to wake us up and put us in action. Whoever *suffers* and *moans* will be found half-asleep; he either has not heard the voice of Pain, or else would not heed.

A very practical example. Suppose we have a headache — the simplest and commonest form of bodily disturbance. The head is our brainhouse, the ache is our unknown friend come to warn us. What do we do? Kill the ache and imagine thereby the head is saved! Headache powders are murderers of our best friend. And even at that, the fire in the head smolders on, to break out afresh in some new spot where we least expect. Chronic dyspepsia, blood-poisoning, deafness, and other severe ailments have been caused by the foolish attempt to kill an ache instead of to remove the trouble.

Let us look further into this matter of headache. It may be caused by one or more of the following things — among others. Weak eyes; bad air; faulty sleep; lack of exercise; artificial heat; excessive use of the brain (rare); local derangement; spinal dislocation; indigestion; liver trouble; undereating or overeating; strain of responsibility or extreme effort; moral delinquency; psychic disorder; intense grief, anxiety or passion; chronic worry, monotony, repression or overstimulation. How does the headache "remedy" perform? Does it remove, or even disclose, the origin of the ill? Rather, it so deadens our sensibilities that we cannot feel the ache — while the cause remains untouched. The cause may be physical, mental, emotional, spiritual — yet the alleged cure is utterly, soddenly, materialistic. Whatever "cures" the pain kills the patient. The only way to rescue the patient is to help him find and treat the cause; but the "cure" for anything only puts the sufferer into a deeper sleep. Pain is a virtue; but the pain-cause and the pain-killer both are vices.

The scientific name for the average semi-invalid is semi-ignoramus or semi-vegetable. The writer knows, because he used to be one. The semiinvalid is usually a person content to remain either ignorant or inactive. When he begins to know, then *do*, he feels his trouble vanishing. But so long as he expects to buy salvation wrapped in a pill, chemical or metaphysical, he voluntarily stultifies his own intelligence, the resulting condition being torpor and stagnation. There are crises when a drug may be invaluable. But the doctor with a training confined entirely to *materia medica* is not a safe practitioner — the mental, emotional and psychic factors in disease are always present, and often more potent than the physiological. Health relates to the whole man — not to his mere body. The millennium will be when our preachers make us well, our doctors make us good, and our teachers make us powerful.

The sick man has broken a divine law of Nature, and is serving out his term of moral punishment. Stop his suffering prematurely and you make him a virtual jail-breaker. As for coddling or parading"symptoms," that is equivalent to showing prison-stripes and being proud of them.

The convict is often punished unjustly — but the invalid never; for the laws of Nature, whose violation brings the penalty of disease, are the direct, original, handiwork of the Creator.

The sanctity of the human body has yet to be realized by civilized people. Most of the things we eat and drink, wear and use and heap around us, rob us of vitality and so of spirituality. The vital is not always spiritual, but the spiritual is always vital. A wholesome religion bears first on the body. No man can be truly good and permit such physical desecration as bolting his food, sleeping in a hot or unaired room, neglecting to exercise, or adopting clothes which to be stylish must be uncomfortable.

Until we learn to identify natural instinct with its Divine Source, we shall go on suffering because we go on sinning. There is no suffering without previous sinning.

Pain shows us where we have been wrong. If we are open-eyed, honest, brave, we gladly receive the warning, thank Pain for the lesson, and by removing the cause make further suffering needless. If we have considered Pain our enemy, we should remember that the object of enemies is to make us friends with ourselves. The truest friendship is to uncover in us the places that need strengthening. And of all our friends, Pain does this best.

Pain, however, is more than a watchman. Pain is a guide to opportunity and a giver of bounty. If we seize all the treasures that Pain holds for us, we find our tears lost amid our blessings.

Pain lengthens life. Who is generally the prey of typhoid fever, apoplexy, and other acute disorders? The fleshy, full-blooded, easy-going man, the man who was "never sick a day in his life." You have to be sick in order to learn how to stay well. People who have had a small fire in one room don't let their house burn down — they buy extinguishers or they get insurance. Most bodies burn out, most brains rust out. Suffering lowers the vital flame and thus prevents a death by sudden conflagration; while the intellect, forced to exert itself, helps the sufferer into a commonsense way of living. Be glad if you're sick — it's good for you. But only as you stop it. The final cure for chronic disease is half-gratitude, half grit.

Pain punctuates pleasure. Did you ever try to read a page of type without capitals or punctuation-marks? Just that sense of irritation and fatigue would accompany a life wholly void of sadness. Joy may write the text of life, but sorrow forms the capitals. And you know a good printer, a fine penman, makes of the capitals the artistic work of the page. Being happy without interruption would seem horribly dull. Fortunately, most of us do not need a warning against the monotony of such a plight — we have an excess of dots and dashes, question-marks and exclamation-points, strewn about, regardless of the meaning.

Pain develops the individual. How did Theodore Roosevelt become the towering figure in world-politics? By dismissing Pain and engaging Pain's twin-sister, *Power*. How did Eugen Sandow become the world's most famous athlete? By turning natural weakness into supernatural strength; by laughing at Pain, conquering Privation, scouting Heredity, and sending all other ghostly worries into everlasting oblivion. You won't see until you suffer. How can you advance until you do? No matter what your trouble is, you can make it a threshold of triumph. That's what trouble is for. And most triumphs were built on that foundation.

Pain empowers the conscience. No man has a healthy conscience until he knows by instinct how to live naturally — hence painlessly. Invalids do things right along to their bodies that they know they shouldn't, often consoling themselves with the outworn delusion that character settles in the soul and never changes the body. A sick body is a soulless body. Spiritual strength demands physical nerve and mental muscle. Can you find real music in a church organ when the reeds are broken and the stops refuse to work? No more can you find real spirituality in a human body when the physical and mental powers, through disuse or abuse, have become incapacitated. Pain reveals how divinity has been thwarted. Sin is the keynote of suffering, but suffering the prelude to sanctity.

Pain refines the sensibilities. We think ourselves intelligent — because forsooth we own a lusty array of bodily senses. We see with our eyes, we hear with our ears, we touch and smell and taste, with all our human functions do we not know? There are vast undiscovered realms of mental, emotional and psychic possibility, lying just beyond our human perceptions. To know anything finally, we must be more than human. All the seers, the martyrs, the creators, the messiahs of the world have risen through anguish into understanding. Our senses, crude as the gold before it meets the fire, must be slowly purified. Grief, white-hot, tempers the soul for immortality. Just before dying, having suffered and waited long, many a weary, tortured soul catches wonderful glimpses of a new, angelic world, rare music from another distant sphere, grows exalted, seems transfigured, shines with a heavenly beauty, partakes of a keener, fuller life in the very throes of what we call death. Perhaps, if we dared suffer while yet able to use the lesson, we should have this ultimate glory to live by instead of to catch on the brink of death.

Pain deepens fellowship. — Did you ever find the key to somebody's heart, then have you crept in silently, softly, taking a place to hold forever? Was not the door of the heart left unguarded in a moment of grief? We are never so human as when we are hurt. And whoever comforts us in our woe makes himself a part of our weal. You may laugh with your gay companions, but when you weep you turn to your mother. Pain, holding a tithe of the agony of motherhood, makes the harshest of us tender, the crudest of us all-for-giving. Smiles may seal friendship, but tears alone cement it.

Pain liberates the soul. The majority of us identify ourselves with our bodies. That is why we fear death. Such a position is both unethical and unscientific. Hypnotism has demonstrated beyond question that the soul is immune to physical suffering, and unconscious of actual torture except through the medium of the brain. You can run knives through the arm of the hypnotic sleeper and never once disturb him — he is disconnected from the part of him that suffers. Now intense hurt of any kind will, after a while, automatically establish a feeling of conscious superiority to physical states. In a word, Pain separates the man from his enfleshment, bestowing a sense of poise, and removing the fear of death. We shrink not from the dissolution of the body, which normally is painless; but from the disintegration of the soul.

As the living soul grows conscious of itself, all thought of death passes. In reality, the death of the body is nothing; for each new growth of mind, heart or spirit follows a new birth, and for every birth we pay with a death. There may be times when the bravest, wisest, truest and only possible thing is to go on suffering with a higher aim in view than ease of mind and body. There is no spiritual exercise equal to that of facing an incurable hurt. The physical cripple often grows soonest into the moral giant. As a soldier, nearing victory, though wounded rushes on, so the moral crusader while afflicted and distressed may yet uphold so earnestly his banner of idealism that he simply does not feel the pangs of battle. Choosing to suffer, because of a principle, has been the part of the world's immortals. Loneliness, misunderstanding, loss of reputation, poverty, endless misery, infinite heartache, persecution, martyrdom — these all are none too great a price for spiritual freedom. Not until we would gladly forfeit all human joys do we know the bliss that hides in the heart of anguish.

CHAPTER 22

When Love Comes

THERE are moments of childhood that seem to the rest of life as radiant jewels miraculously strewn above a dull background of common clay. These ptecious moments form the diadem of memory which in the dark after-years we may cherish and restore, to prove that we are of royal birth.

This gleaming crown of childhood holds for me an opal hour. Other shining bits of memory have become as sapphire, pearl or ruby in the golden strand of childish reminiscence. But this was the opal hour, the hour of matchless beauty when all the blended colors of a new world of light surpassed mortal vision, to challenge and inspire imagination.

Have you ever stood at a great height, and for the first time overlooked the world? Then you will know what I mean by the opal hour.

Perhaps too you may recall the dark, earthen hours that lay between you and the height. So you can follow me, as we trace our path in the journey of that summer's day, twenty years ago.

We were camping at the foot of a deep wild canyon, where the whisper of the trees and the echo of the whip-poor-will filled the wooded valley with melody. A murmuring mountain stream with its low caressing song soothed us to sleep at nightfall. But the vision of the dawn was a rugged sight of grandeur; for the mountain rose sheer three thousand feet above us, and the misty, cloud-veiled summit piercing the golden sky held us enthralled, till we could resist no longer.

A narrow path — dim, steep, long and arduous, was the only means of ascent. This we entered early one morning, following the guidance of the man in the party who had scaled the peak and could show us the way. Each had to climb alone, for the tangled spiny arms of underbrush creeping everywhere through the forest almost closed above our path. The foliage grew so dense and the way so winding that only the voice of the guide, shouting in advance of unexpected turns, kept us all together in safety.

We were in perpetual twilight, except for a little rift of sunshine that broke now and then through our vaulted roof of interlaced branches. Strange birds cried and fled in the darkness, terrified at the sound of human voices. Unseen animals crashed through the boughs, forced in angry mood from their lair; and the timid ones among us turned white with fear. Once the head of a great serpent darted from beneath an overjutting rock, hissing defiance as we hurried past.

Huge boulders lay athwart our advance; deep crevasses yawned ahead, bridged only with a treacherous, hollow, moss-grown log; at last we crawled on hands and knees through a grim city of caverns, silently feeling our way in the gloom by the touch of the cold rock-walls dripping moisture from the underworld and buried in the shadows of the centuries. Here the weak among us turned back;

trembling with fright, bruised and weary, wondering if we were not lost, a few of the party halted in dismay, while the rest pushed on.

But the hardest of the climb was over — such a little while and the path led us out on a broad plateau where the beauty of Nature and the majesty of God seemed to meet half way between earth and heaven, and to open wide a new, clear vista of larger understanding. The platform of rock on which we stood overhung the valley three thousand feet below. From the brink of the ledge the river wound like a mere thread of silver, and our camp was a tiny white spot on a boundless horizon of verdure and sky. We were neighbors to only the eagles, calmly soaring in space. All sense of human weakness and limitation vanished; we became to ourselves heirs of the heavens, wielding dominion over the ages, sharing the rule and the plan of the Infinite Mind. In that one hour of revelation we grew, spiritually, to a nobler stature than years of earth-bound life had produced.

And, from the summit, we caught a glimpse of a shorter, easier path down the slope; — you that scorn poetry because it isn't useful!

This day was an allegory, symbolic of human experience. The gloom and toil and hardship of an endless upward climb is all we see in life — until a memory or hope of a perfect love at the summit leads us out in triumph above a world's despair. When this love comes, we can look back and smile at the trivial, momentary, oppositions — the boulders of difficulty, the tangles of doubt, the serpents of anxiety, the wild beasts of enmity, the inclines of error, the steeps of delay. For, at the zenith of love, the purpose of all things is written, on the broad scroll of the heavens in gleaming letters of light. Toward this vision, to this eminence, all human life is directed. Those who grieve, who complain, who err, who grow impatient, have but paused for a moment in their upward journey whose end will be the perfect joy of knowing through loving. The love-life is perpetual dawn — all other life perpetual midnight. By this we may know why our way is clouded; we simply do not love enough.

The scientific world is now recognizing the practical value of sentiment in everyday life. Suggestion or auto-suggestion, which is being used by all advanced physicians, and investigated by many clergymen, teachers and business men, is only a popular form of idealism or transcendentalism. Delicate instruments have been devised to weigh thoughts and analyze emotions. There are even those who claim to have photographed prayers at the moment of ascension.

All this is commonplace to the student of esoteric principles. For the mystics and seers of the Orient have long known the psychic nature and origin of the material body, and have classified human desires into visible shapes and colors.

But the greatest discovery is yet to come. Namely this: that all human action is based on human love; and that the solar plexus, which is the *source* of motive, must be educated in advance of the brain, which is merely the receptacle of *method*. Those who perform great deeds act out what they *feel*. Every colossal figure in history has been moved by an overwhelming love. What the race needs most is to understand the emotions, passions, and desires which lead either to superhuman effort and achievement — or to ruin and despair. Wisdom may be stored in the mind, but destiny is molded in the heart.

There can be nothing more fundamental, more practical, more scientific, than love. We are told that the first law of life is self-preservation, and the second law self-perpetuation. True enough; but what animates and regulates both these laws is the kind and amount of love in your heart — love for self, and love for the human family. The sick man is always deficient in self-love. And the unwise, inefficient or complaining mother is lacking in love for children. That which we love we unconsciously exalt. And the cure for most human ills is exaltation. A physiological statement that any thoughtful doctor will verify.

For common disorders of the system, the custom is nowadays to prescribe a form of massage, hydropathy, electricity, gymnastics, or special diet. Why? Because these natural agencies relieve congestion, promote combustion and expel impurities by increasing the vibration of the bodycells. *Affection does the same thing;* any man, woman or child who loves deeply enough automatically increases the vibration of the whole organism to such a pitch that only health is possible. Love work, love play, love food, love exercise, love air and sun and water, love books, love ideals, love some one as a reason for loving all these other things; — and you have the knowledge of perennial health, the secret of immortal youth.

The phrase "warm-hearted" is more than a figure of speech. The action of your heart, the strength of your lungs, the tone of your digestion and the rate of your blood supply depend on the vigor of your love-nature and its honest expression. Thousands of over-worked men, hundreds of thousands of nervous women, want not so much *recreation* as the *re-creation* of a strong, pure, devout love. The ocean voyage recommended by the doctor is to separate you from that which you do not love. He won't tell you this — he can't afford to. But if you will take my word in time, you can save that expense.

Go to the other extreme — the idealistic. Ask why we all love such different things, different people, different modes of activity and spheres of life. The answer: *We love most that which will soonest perfect us.* Hence the only way for loved ones to be loyal to each other is to rival each other in growth. Incidentally, the proof of our love is how we develop in the absence of the loved one. You butterfly women who fear the loss of your husband's love while you take your summer's jaunt alone; — you have nothing to fear, because you have nothing to lose. The man who can't be trusted is artificially tied; and the wife had better look to her own heart-strings. Each sex is responsible for the wounds inflicted by the other; hence recrimination is absurd, and the alleged conflict between them, painted so vividly by G. Bernard Shaw in testimony of his penprowess, resolves to nothing but a crude, flamboyant advertisement.

We love most that which will soonest perfect us. The romantic young girl is wildly enamored of the eloquent poet, the skilled musician, dispassionate actor. She cannot express the cravings and emotions she feels — therefore she worships him who can. But if she marries the poet, musician or actor — woe be to her! For what she needs then is a knowledge of how to go marketing, wash dishes and make dresses; and the man she worships then must have the money to buy these things done. You cannot satisfy a woman short of perfection; and if you were perfect, you would not be interesting. The reason lovers are in Heaven is because only Heaven knows what to do with them. If earth knew, earth would be Heaven. And the pity, the tragedy, of earth is that here lovers are so often out of place. Lovers wear a halo that makes everything look different. The halo is the realest thing about them; but those who do not love cannot see —? all they have to guide them is the touch of the blind.

Love should be synonymous with life. We live only as long, and as much, as we love. Indeed, the love of love supplants the love of life, in the highest forms of growth. Birds have been known to die of loneliness and grief, when their mates had gone. A common dog, of ordinary faithfulness, will guard his master's life and property with no thought of his own comfort or even safety. Dumb animals often shame us by their whole-hearted love and loyalty.

All genius bears tribute to the inevitable conquest of life by love. The man with a message gladly starves that the child of his brain and heart may come into being — every man with a message is more woman than man. The true mother, whose highest anguish and ecstasy reaches the plane of genius, exults in death if only her babe may live. The martyr, the warrior, the devout man of science or medicine, faces annihilation unconscious of the danger, lost in the love of a great purpose or a sublime truth. We are none of us grown till death for the sake of love is more appealing than life for the sake of living.

But the animating power of an all-absorbing love does not wait for the unusual, the heroic, the impossible; rather it fills the smallest things of life with a meaning so tremendous that smallness disappears. We love in proportion as we grow alert in little things. You may find a goldmine on your sweetheart's birthday — and to her it means nothing if you forget the birthday. Whereas, you may go broke and she will still call you the dearest thing in the world if you spend your last nickel on a flower to symbolize the sweetness of the day. How to hold a wife's love: Watch out for the little things. Love's crucial test for a man is to keep his sensibilities fine — Love's crucial test for a woman is to keep her sympathies true.

When Love comes, what happens?

Everything goes that hinders unfoldment, harmony and happiness. The going may be gradual, but you can fairly see the change in your life, work and character.

When Love comes, Doubt goes. We are ignorant, and perplexed, only because we fail to live out the most and best we know. Can you imagine a rose perturbing itself with metaphysical arguments, political dissensions, or theological hair-splittings? The rose lives for just one purpose — to express its own beauty and fragrance. Love liberates all the hidden beauty and fragrance in the human soul; and the soul, as the flower, establishes itself wherever allowed to unfold. Only our restrictions perplex us.

When Love comes, Deceit goes. Do you want an infallible way to prove your love for a man or a maid? It is this: that in the presence of your real sweetheart you must reveal everything, share everything, count everything dear only as divided. There is nothing more false, nor more insidiously harmful, than the idea that a man to enjoy himself must lie to his wife. So-called jokes based on this fallacy are equivalent to mental, moral and psychic murder. When the human race has approached something like intelligence, we shall prohibit by law the appearance in newspapers or on the stage of marital infelicity jests, because to the social body they are as deadly as plague-spots. Just to the degree that we love do our lives become limpid sweet and crystal clear; deception cannot remain, any more than stagnation and decay could persist on the surface of a rippling mountain stream.

When Love comes, Folly goes. Have you never seen a butter-fly-woman gladly fold her wings and assume the burdens of a house-hold — because the love of husband and babies made her freer than she had been with all her careless flitting? The recognition of a personal ideal makes irresponsibility unthinkable forever after. Love means whole-souled admiration; and all mistakes occur when we are moving away from what we admire. Does your boy find more trouble in a day than you can get him out of in a week? Then you do some finding — you find where his admiration lies, appeal to his hero-worship, put him on his mettle to equal in solid worth the object of his affection. Erring is only forgetting what or whom we adore.

When Love comes, Pride goes. The man proud of achievements, the woman proud of appearances, is merely a victim of the micro-scopehabit, and needs a horizon for a cure. What we have done, been, learned, suffered and conquered is so infinitesimal beside our future possibilities that recollection itself becomes a confession and irritation. Infinitely daring, yet infinitely humble; this Love makes us while we view the remoteness of our own ideal and the perfection of the loved one whose inspiration urges on to the farthest goal. Purpose consumes pride; and to love is to be all purpose.

When Love comes, Weakness goes. Human energy is a form of electricity, and the dynamo is charged with affection. Every tiny thrill of sentiment adds to the storage-power of your energy machine called the body. When these thrills are sufficient in number and strength you will be fighting-mad all the time — if that is the mood you need in which to conquer all that stands between you and your love. The only thing a lover can't do is to say Can't!

When Love comes, Selfishness goes. The joy of giving up exceeds the pleasure of possessing as the heavens exceed the earth. There is perhaps only one joy greater — that of gaining for the sake of giving up, of struggling and winning just to lay down the laurels at the feet of a loved one. This really is the highest form of selfhood or true selfishness; since what we idolize prophesies what we shall be, and to sacrifice for those we love is but to hasten our own advance. Only those talk of self-denial who have failed of self-discovery.

When Love comes, Age goes. This is the crowning miracle of life; that in a genuine love, the purity and faith of childhood is blended with the valor and wisdom of middle-age, giving to those who attain this love a spirit of immortal youth molded by a knowledge of worldly experience. None can love and remain ignorant — none can love and become coarse. The glorious mystic dawn of creation lends perpetual light, with the strength of the morning, to those who esteem their love before all else. Weariness, discouragement, disillusionment, wait for him who treads a loveless path; but neither time can dull nor space deter nor even death alter the endless reality of progress and communion that souls feel who love altogether. Convinced by their own sureness of the ultimate goodness of things, looking at the play of life serene with a cloudless consciousness, trusting and hoping and working and waiting, they who love can face together all the woes of a world of sense — and only smile toward the vision of permanence beyond.

THE END

EFFICIENT LIVING

(Available soon at TriumphBookPress.com)

EFFICIENT LIVING

BY

EDWARD EARLE PURINTON

Author of "The Triumph of the Man Who Acts," etc.

Director of the Efficiency Service of

THE INDEPENDENT

NEW YORK

ROBERT M. McBRIDE & COMPANY

1915

CONTENTS

CHAPTER I

WHAT IS EFFICIENCY?

RECENTLY I talked with the highest-salaried man in the world. I asked him how he had succeeded.

He quietly answered, "I haven't succeeded. No real man ever succeeds. There is always a larger goal ahead."

This multi-millionaire has outrun every rival on earth. But he has not reached the goal of his own satisfaction. He is an efficient man. Efficiency begins with wanting something so hard the whole world can't stop you.

Efficiency is new, and all new things are misunderstood. Conversing with an anarchistic labor leader, I chanced to mention the topic. He snorted his sentiments. "I hate the very word," he rampaged. "The idea of ticketing and marketing a man by how many motions an hour he can make, is a blot on the American flag," he exclaimed patriotically. Then he begged me to aid his cause with a few dollars that I had made by studying efficiency.

Efficiency is the difference between wealth and poverty, fame and obscurity, power and weakness, health and disease, growth and death, hope and despair. Efficiency makes kings of us all.

Only efficiency conquers fate. Every man's life is a battle ground, with fate and efficiency struggling for possession. Fate is against him, efficiency for him, and all the man's forces are lined up on one side or the other. Where do you stand? Have you marshaled your thoughts, acts and emotions under efficiency's banner? If not, prepare to be assailed, overwhelmed and dismembered by fate.

Efficiency tells us how great men have won their battle with fate, and how we can win ours. Efficiency leads us from a world of chance to a realm of choice, changing us from automatons to men. Efficiency provides our only freedom—that of shaping circumstances and hewing events to suit ourselves!

Look back ten years. Think what you have paid for experience. If you had known then what you know to-day, how much time, health, money, faith, energy, you could have saved. Efficiency offers the only short cut to experience by showing us what other men, similarly placed, have learned and done and been.

What is efficiency?

It is not motion-study, or vocation-test, or cost-saving, or any other mechanical thing. It is not an effort of greedy corporations to reduce their workers to money-making machines. It is not a panic to do so much that you wear yourself out.

Efficiency is the science of self-management.

We have none of us learned it. We feed our kine properly—and dig our own graves with our teeth. We curry our horses beautifully—and neglect to take baths enough to keep us well. We exercise our pet poodle daily—and pant for breath if we run a block. We oil our engines wisely—and allow rust to gather on our brain. We demand a perfect telegraph system—and let our nerves run wild. Man is the only machine we have never learned how to use.

For our ignorance, we pay. It is estimated that seventy-three men out of every hundred are in the wrong job; that most men utilize only about a third of their mental and spiritual forces; that the average American family could live on what they waste; that our business firms lose $100,000,000 a year through ineffective advertising; that in the United States there are always 3,000,000 persons on the sick list; that the number of preventable deaths each year is 630,000; that the annual waste from preventable death and disease is $1,500,000,000; and that somewhere in this country a workman is being killed every four minutes, and another being injured every four seconds! Do we not need efficiency?

The American slogan is efficiency. We aim at world-supremacy. And the world-master must be first a self-master.

England has had the efficient navy, Germany the efficient army, France the efficient household, Italy the efficient art, Japan the efficient hygiene, Scotland the efficient thrift, New Zealand the efficient government. And America? The efficient nerve. We will try anything, and try for anything. Our destiny lies in our daring. Our nation's flag is the Stars and Stripes, because we aim at the stars—and smile at the stripes!

But we waste more than we use—more money, more strength, more time, more thought, more opportunity. We must learn conservation and direction through efficiency. Then we shall rule the world—if we deem it worth ruling.

I was going to ask, "Are you efficient?" But, on second thought, I see how vain it would be. The only person who knows all about a man is his office-boy, and the only person who knows all about a lady is her kitchen-maid. I assume that you are neither the office-boy nor the kitchen-maid; so why bother you with foolish questions? A better method—a scientific test—herewith appears.

It is safe to conclude that, if you are engaged in a large enterprise, and have not applied efficiency methods to yourself and your associates, you are losing from $1,000 to $100,000 a year. If you are an individual, professional or industrial worker, your loss will perhaps run from $100 to $5,000 a year. Why go on wasting this money?

The difference between a hod-carrier and the head of a million-dollar corporation is that the hod-carrier works his hod instead of his head. For the hod he has trained his muscles, to the hod he is bound. To get ahead—get a head! The leader of men has trained not only his muscles, but as well his nerves, his brain, his lungs and pores and organs of digestion, his thoughts, actions and emotions, his instincts, habits, aims and ambitions, his financial status and his moral sinew.

How does the prize athlete gain his laurels? By setting a fixed goal, curbing his appetites and passions, living on the scant fare of the "training table," combining rigid self-control with huge self-exertion. The game of business, the game of life, demands as much. And efficiency sets the training table for the man who is going to be a mental, financial or spiritual leader.

Efficiency is the power of doing one's most and best, in the shortest time and easiest way, to the satisfaction of all concerned.

I put this in italics, to make it stand out. And I would recommend that every so-called "efficiency expert" swiftly and humbly paste it in his hat. Your work is not done when you go into a corporation and show the president how to save a million dollars a year. Efficiency is more than speed and economy—it is the reeducation and reconstruction of men. No worker is efficient until he would rather work than eat. Man is both a machine and a spirit. You've got to reach the spirit side, to make the machine go. The greatest corporations are doing this, and the success of modern institutions like the National Cash Register Company and the New York Edison Company lies in their habit of making their workers bigger men while making them better machines.

Are you doing your most and best? Do you execute your work in the shortest possible time and the easiest known way? Is everybody satisfied with results—from president to office-boy, including clerks, clients, competitors, and your folks at home? If so, then you are 100 per cent efficient—kindly hand this article to a neighbor who needs it. (You will have no trouble finding him, because you are the only man in the world who is perfect on all these five points.)

The efficient person feels that he can do anything—but that he has done nothing. When I see the average "self-made" man, pompous and fat and wheezy, I with difficulty restrain myself from laughing impolitely. He looks like a house with the roof blown off, and half the basement caved in. An efficient man, like an efficient house, has four sides. His body forms the foundation, his mind the outer walls, his heart the inner hangings and treasures and pictures, his soul the gable-windows, the tower and the roof. To be merely an intellectual or financial giant is to be the hulk of a man. Efficiency must build on a splendid physique, and must crown its work with a spiritual faith. A dyspeptic is a house with no foundation, an agnostic is a house with no roof.

Now for a practical, personal example. I know a man who has increased by about 500 per cent his daily output of work, his optimism and will power, his health reserve and his financial resourcefulness. Let me tell how he did it.

First. He analyzed himself. He discovered what he most wanted to do and have and be, in life. He was not dismayed by the fact that his desires looked about as unattainable as the moon. He said nothing, and took the next step. (What makes a dream visionary is not the dream but the do-lessness of the dreamer.)

Second. He studied his possibilities and limitations, physical, mental and spiritual. By consulting authorities on athletics, higher metaphysics, vocational training, physiognomy and experimental psychology, he learned that his ambitions lay within the reach of his natural gifts. (We may remark in passing that these methods of character reading are not infallible, and few of their exponents are reliable; they contain, however, sufficient truth to make them valuable in choosing a career.)

Third. He read the lives of the world's great man who had been leaders in his chosen field. He formed the acquaintance of living leaders, through mutual friends. He saw that he was out of gear in certain ways—and he proceeded to repair his faulty machinery, of body, brain, equipment and environment.

Fourth. He resigned his position in a dignified profession; and got a menial, trivial job that paid next to nothing. The job was in line with his goal—the profession was not. And $5 a week in a place with an open door is a better wage than $50 a week in a place that leads nowhere.

Fifth. He made the most of his job. The men who look for a job are so many because the men who look into a job are so few. Every job is a gold-mine of possibility; but you must work it by seeking and digging in your spare time. This youth took up motion-study, time-study, tool-study, and other methods of modern "scientific management." He learned to save two hours a day, which he spent in talking with men higher up, in reading trade books and magazines, in experimenting on ways of improving his work, and in planning his line of advance.

Sixth. He observed that he was handicapped by the presence of chronic ailments and disorders, which resulted in fatigue, headache, irritability, auto-intoxication, and other hindrances to good work. He studied hygiene, found that no disease is incurable, stopped the use of drugs, changed his methods of eating, began to take regular exercise and a morning sponge, kept his chamber window wide open, did a few more sensible things that most people don't do till they have to—and presently watched his troubles disappear. By adopting health habits, he increased the daily output of energy at least 200 per cent and got so much more done.

Seventh. He changed his mind. This man was naturally a pessimist and grumbler, harsh, cruel, hasty, blunt, surrounding himself with enemies and worries. Gaining sense enough to see what a fool he had been, he applied himself to a systematic cultivation of optimism, faith, tact, patience, tolerance, courtesy, and other mental factors in efficiency. Having grown friendly minded, he attracted thousands of friends. And his work prospered accordingly.

Eighth. He arranged to secure the best available cooperation, financial, industrial and moral support, from his associates inside and outside the business.

Ninth. He discerned that specific moral qualities were needed in him to produce leadership; so he developed courage, will power, conviction, enthusiasm, inspiration—as athletes develop physical muscles.

Tenth. He married the woman of his heart, and she made him do the impossible, to reach her ideal of strength and wisdom in a man. (This was not a part of his efficiency scheme. In order to be sure they will get discipline the good Lord lets men think they are marrying for happiness—else would they never marry.)

The result? A few years ago this man's wages were $4 a week and board. He is to-day master of three different lines of work, any one of which would yield a splendid income. And the mental and moral gains have been even greater.

Now for the application. You and I can't follow the particular method of any other man on earth; but we can recognize the scientific principles in the foregoing history and apply them in our way.

The first move toward efficiency is to find how much we need it. When a man's grade falls below 80 per cent in college, he is considered a poor student, either very lazy or very dull. Yet in the appended self-examination for the school of life, not one person in a hundred reaches 80 per cent. Go over the questions and figure out where you stand. Then give a copy of the Test to each member of your family, club, class or business organization. Properly used, the Test is worth more than a year of academic study, which costs perhaps $500.

I judge that on this Test the average grade is 40 per cent.

This means that the $40-a-week man could, and should, earn $100—and then be less tired and worried than he is now. What is your income? What might it be, on this ratio? Efficiency measure is money, and every item of this Test has a money value.

But the efficient man does not put money first. The pulse of the battle, with Fate and surroundings and himself; the call of an unconquered world to gigantic effort; the inspiration of heroic deeds by other men; the might of self-rule, and the joy of self-expression; the loves of the heart and the longings of the soul; the far, lone gleam of destiny; these things nerve and impel the efficient man to do always more and be always greater.

Magnificent possibilities lie unexplored, undiscovered, unimagined, within the mental recesses and spiritual treasure-troves common to us all. Only a crisis—a great responsibility, a matchless opportunity, a sudden death or disaster—avails to rouse and develop these unused powers. Lacking the crisis, we are prone to sleep or fritter our lives away.

The transcendental problem of humanity is to be as great always as one can be at rare moments. Men are as great as they force themselves to use themselves. Genius is but an irresistible urge to be occupied. The man who succeeds has become a self-winding watch on his own movements, so that he knows by intuition when he is either running down or wearing himself out. Starvation is the best remedy for under-action, sleep the best remedy for over-action.

There is no error unattended by repression. We make mistakes because we are deficient in the power to see, or in the power to do as we see. But spiritual sight and sinew may be cultivated, will be cultivated systematically in the ages to come. The time is fast approaching when only a spiritual Hercules can move the world. Mental giants rule now, but their crude force merely corresponds to the primitive condition of the race. First body-rule, now brain-rule, next heart-rule, finally soul-rule; this is the plan of world-sovereignty.

What are some of the unused powers that we own but do not turn to advantage?

Unused muscles, unused lungs, unused instincts, unused emotions, unused perceptions, unused faculties, unused ideals. We say nothing of unused stomachs or of unused tongues. If exercise alone could keep us healthy, the stomach and the tongue would exhibit so blithe a vigor that all meandering microbes would flee in disgust. (If you expected here only a sermon, and object to the ghost of a smile that may have come flitting across the horizon, please remember that of all our unused powers, none more fully repays conscientious development than our somewhat timorous sense of humor.)

Unused muscles cripple us. Not externally, but vitally. If you ever witnessed the marvelous feats performed by Sandow or any other "strong man," you know what a beautiful network of muscles envelop and support the fine torso of the trained athlete—his body is a work of art. But do you know that his superb digestion is maintained largely by these interlaced muscular fibers, which hold the digestive organs in true position, thus enabling them to act freely? Are you anaemic, thin, troubled with poor circulation? Then look to the muscles of arms and legs; for live blood follows live muscles, and where there is weak assimilation there is weak sinew. So apparently remote a thing as sleep is affected by muscular condition; if your sleep is fitful, and your body tied in a bow-knot, your back muscles and shoulder muscles need attention—their flabbiness permits the spine to crook and the chest to sag, hence the nerves cannot relax nor the blood circulate. Withered muscles work havoc throughout the whole system.

Unused lungs cripple us. The majority of civilized people exert only a fraction of their normal breathing capacity; and a host of ills, from brain-fag and ennui to dyspepsia, come from this defect in respiration. Great singers, champion swimmers, and other such lung-developers, are usually marvels of robustness. On taking sudden exercise, do you feel dizziness, vertigo, or rush of blood to the head. Then your lung chambers have been short of oxygen, since the effort to fill them causes unaccustomed pressure, which you feel accordingly. How long can you hold your breath without discomfort? If for a minute or longer, you may be glad of a pair of lungs that know their business and stick to it. The lungs are the organs of liberation; exercised deeply and regularly, they free us mentally and spiritually as well as physically. Conquerors have often been men of small stature—but of gigantic breathing power. From Cromwell on the battlefield to Beecher in the pulpit, the takers of the world's citadels have found their source of power in the breath.

Unused instincts cripple us. The instinct of the animal guards him against foes, against poisons, against all outer perils known or unknown. At the approach of danger, the snail retreats into his shell, the porcupine bristles, the deer flees with the wind. Yet we, who are supposed to know more, do less. We regularly eat what we know isn't good for us, allowing poison, in quality or quantity, to enter the system through the mouth; we are guided by appetite instead of by hunger; we choke our food down when we should rest and ruminate; we add tonics and peptonizers to the gastronomic insult— then we sadly complain how afflicted we are with a poor stomach! Moreover, we entertain as regular guests such thoughts as lead to mental paralysis and spiritual decrepitude —worry, fear, jealousy, doubt, dependence, deceit, compromise. The snail, the deer and the porcupine would do it better—in the presence of such intruders we must cultivate our shell, our sinews of flight, or our bristles if need be.

Unused emotions cripple us. The height of our attainment is directly proportioned to the depth of our feeling. All great men have one trait in common; a fierce intensity, which annihilates all things superficial and irrelevant. Convention forbids this—convention thrives on pettiness. It is not "good form" to feel deeply; it is good form to die prematurely, the coffin is the symbol of good form. So long as the favorite disease of fashion is repression, so long will nerves be the favorite symptoms of fashion. We might almost say that no man is healthy who has not experienced a sublime joy or an over-whelming sorrow. Our emotions extend us into a realm divine, the knowledge of which provides our human lives with infinite capacity for growth. To feel deeply is to understand the world, to feel nobly is to penetrate the heavens; to feel strongly is to force Fate.

Unused perceptions cripple us. Until we escape the dominion of the senses, we dwell in chaos personified. That is why the Oriental mystic refuses to converse, to eat, to shake hands, to see his friends, to enjoy music or perfume—until his outer senses have been silenced, that his inner sensibilities may be uttered. The self-banishment of Tolstoi on the eve of death, after his self-deprivation through life, was but an echo of the world-old cry of the soul to be loosed from the flesh, and perceive more clearly with the trammels gone. We cannot all be sages, seers or mystics, we have work to do on the earth-plane; but we can all recognize the presence of finer forces about it, and so attune ourselves as to hear and voice in our own way the heavenly strains of the Great Monition. You tell me that prayer exalts the soul? I tell you that prayer clears the eye, steadies the hand, calms the nerve, quickens the judgment, strengthens the will, makes the whole man keen, alert, and sure. The non-religious man is a dwarf in his subjective nature. He is to be pitied, not condemned.

Unused faculties cripple us. What can we do best? Are we doing it? Can we find in our work full scope and play for our talents? Are we consciously progressing every day toward a fixed goal? These questions are of life -long and earth-wide importance. Every human being is a conglomeratlon of plus and minus qualities, which must be classified, arranged, unified, before the personal equation is solved. There should be in every college a department of Character Study, devoted to the recognition, measurement and equalization of the strong and weak faculties of the youth who attend. The only drawback would be that the man able to run this department couldn't be held in a college—the corporations would get him at $50,000 or so a year! The warrior is weak in Ideality, the poet weak in Continuity, the pedagogue weak in Combativeness, the hermit weak in Sociability, the cynic weak in Hope. Yet each is strong in his own peculiar field. The problem of life is so to choose our field that our strength may be apparent.

Unused ideals cripple us. An ideal is a premonition of power. The idealist often squanders or fails to use his power—then the onlooker blames the ideal. There is nothing so dangerous to the spiritual life as to conceive an ideal, undertake a pilgrimage for it, then turn back.

It is like entering a path over a chasm so narrow and steep that one false step means destruction, and you have not time to pause, or room to retreat. These are the marching orders given the idealist: "On and up—or die!" Remain blind, if you will, to your own possibilities on earth, and the glories of the heavens beyond. But having sought your vision, and beheld one thing clearly, follow that to the end. Nothing worse than death awaits. And to fall amid the peaks, with the sun full upon you, is a death that angels might envy.

"How then may we find and free ourselves?"

Perhaps you are asking this—every honest thinker must ask it sooner or later.

There is no easy way, no quick way, no cheap way. The effective way is hard, and long, and painful. But all the great souls who ever lived have trod this way. And the greater the soul, the greater the willingness.

Not long since, Thomas A. Edison was asked to explain his wonderful success. The kernel of his answer lay in one sentence: "The hardest way is almost invariably the best way." He went on to explain that whenever he achieved a result quickly and easily, he at once suspected its genuineness and proceeded to try a different method. Perhaps the first rule for the discovery of talent may be this: Always choose the hardest thing.

Associate with people who have developed themselves, who have done things, not merely have things. The social climber is right in method, if not in motive; the way to get ahead is to follow those who have arrived. Do you enjoy being with those who you know are superior to yourself? Then your powers are in line for development.

But call no man your superior, call the man ahead merely your predecessor; call yourself as great as the greatest, then live up to the acclamation.

Be much alone. Solitude is the birthplace of strong ideas, fine plans and healthy purposes.

Ask some kind friend to tell you exactly what he thinks of you. Double his praise and his censure. Then you will get a fair idea both of what you may become, and of what you now are. No friend ever saw our best—or dared paint our worst.

Keep in touch with the current literature of your business or profession. If you are a merchant or a metaphysician, a doctor or a manufacturer, a housewife or a teacher, there are books and magazines being published that would greatly expedite your work by suggesting ways to economize your expenditure of time, thought and money. Whatever vocation you pursue, keep in touch with the best minds and let your brain be constantly sharpened with new ideas from any source available.

Learn to save motions in your work. This will give you time for something more valuable than work.

Acquire mastery of one thing at a time. It is a joy to master words, a joy to master thoughts, a joy to master acts, a joy to master feelings, a joy to master events, a joy to master people. But each of these forms of mastery is a study in itself; whoever is a graduate in one branch of mastery should forthwith enter another.

Make a thorough, systematic, persistent study of the opportunities around you. Discontented people are merely blind. There are gates opening all the time, which the majority do not see because they are looking at the stars or in the mud. A willingness to face life clears away most of the shadows that obscure life's meaning.

Have faith in your dream. It is the seed of your destiny, let no gust of Fate sweep it away, no man despoil you of it, no battle crush it. Out of dreams grow empires.

Most of all, discover where your genius lies—then follow this path till you reach greatness. Make this your first business, outside of earning your living. Efficiency is primarily a study of human desires, an exploration of human powers, a training of human faculties and a massing of human efforts. Genius is the guiding force back of all this.

We know how to weigh our sugar and salt, how to measure our hats and bedposts, how to drive our teams and trolleys—but the elements of genius that are born in every one of us we sadly ignore, appraising them in neither value, extent nor control. When a man builds a great fortune, or writes a great book, or achieves a great character, we then behold the results of his work and surfeit him with praise. But what he needed was to be understood, loved and helped while he was painfully toiling in the dark. To measure a man's capacities and instruct or inspire him in the training of them—this is the highest form of brotherly kindness.

I suppose that in every group of twenty average people, from three to seven would attain a preeminent success, if they knew where and how to direct their talents. And the others, possessing the same knowledge, would enjoy a success for greater than their present realization. But our systems of education, society, politics, economics, and religion are devised to perpetuate mediocrity —they have no place for genius. So, when the spirit of genius animates a youth, he becomes a rebel. And as a rebel he is feared, hunted, slain.

The first question that I would by law force all prospective teachers, doctors, ministers and parents to answer fully would be this: "How will you recognize, locate and develop the signs and promises of genius in the children under your care?" For it is the child's stupid caretakers who make the stupid child. One of the interesting, pathetic and absurd phenomena in the life of a genius occurs when he visits the place of his birth, and notes with amusement the sleepy-eyed whispers, long-eared head-shakings, and wigwaggings of the same old gawks that live in his home town. They "can't see yet what is in the feller! Hain't he riz in the world—must hev been some fool luck!"

It is never safe to think we know a child. For that which we condemn and punish in the child may be his source of power.

Backwardness is often genius. Minds are of two kinds—porous and retentive. The porous mind absorbs—and exudes—rapidly; it is the mind of the so-called "brilliant" scholar. The retentive mind absorbs slowly—and holds for later use. Thus George Eliot, James J. Hill, and many other types of genius were never heard of till after they were thirty-five, at which age the work of one's life is supposed to be established and productive. By similar token the "prize pupil" often ends in a clerkship—he used his mind for a sieve while in college, and the world doesn't want that variety.

Failure is often genius. The soul of genius is too broad, too versatile, for close confinement in a mere "job." So, until the man of genius discovers himself, he may flounder hopelessly while his dray-horse brethren apparently get ahead. Ulysses S. Grant was a "failure" in the classroom—and a genius on the field of battle. Nearly always, the depth of a failure foreshadows the height of some victory—to the man who never despairs but keeps on climbing. Most people are satisfied with ready-made jobs; but the patrician mind waits a little longer and has a better job made to order.

Crime is often genius. We had a boy in our college who was forever "into all kinds of devilment," according to the statement of a pious professor. This youth was at the bottom of all the mischief in the neighborhood. He was a great explorer of forbidden things. The reformers strove in vain to tie his hands with mental and moral prohibitions. When he left college, with a reputation tarnished but a wit resplendent, he gravitated to a Government Experiment Station. Shortly he became known as a genius in examining, analyzing and classifying all kinds of soils, for the benefit of the farmers. And in the work he loved, his character was redeemed.

Poverty is often genius. The exceptional man is not allowed to make money in ordinary ways, lest he bury his talent in a grave of gold. Therefore he who starves may only be preparing to do a greater thing than the rich man ever dreamed. The most fertile brains, like the most prolific goldfields, may be the last to be discovered.

Idleness is often genius. All great achievements are drawn first in dreams, by the pen of imagination, in the colors of desire. To scoff at the dreamer is to prove oneself a dolt in the psychology of efficiency. While Newton was formulating the discovery of the law of gravitation, the neighbors deplored his folly in thus wasting his time. To be wholly understood is to be proved common. And to be unwilling ever to dream and drift and let the world go by, is to be robbed of the forces and flashlight of genius.

Invalidism is often genius. The robust are seldom great—unless they developed their robustness. Fine talents go with a sensitive, nervous temperament, and a physical machinery overdelicate. The swine seldom needs a doctor—the canary often does. Moreover, physical infirmities add to spiritual powers. Robert Louis Stevenson became a great writer because he was softened and sweetened and calmed and attuned by prolonged suffering and the willingness to bear it bravely. Most of the world-winners have had a physical or mental handicap to goad them on.

Stupidity is often genius. A dynamo and a dust-pan do not work in the same way. A man with a dust-pan mind can be stuffed with ancient, irrelevant, compulsory facts—and be graded 99 per cent in scholarship. But the man with a dynamo mind will not stand for any such insult. I had a college friend who was the object of much pity and not a little ridicule. He simply could not "get his lessons." He was a leader in fraternal, musical and athletic circles—but his teachers passed him for graduation only because he was "such a well-meaning boy, though horribly stupid." Ha! And then again ha! ha! That boy today is vice-president and general manager of the largest concern of its kind in the world, with a salary said to be from $60,000 a year upwards. He is a genius—he was called a fool.

Incorrigibility is often genius. You can dam up a freshet in Spring—but you may expect the stream to burst its banks and flood the surrounding meadows. The child with overflowing spirits who is barricaded by injunctions and threats may become "incorrigible"—as the freshet does. But who blames the freshet? In a town near New York there was recently a wayward lad—the "bad boy" of the village—who for years had been the despair of teachers, doctors, ministers and parents, alike. His pranks were fiendishly cruel—but so fiendishly clever that he could not be caught and punished. He was the Jesse James of the neighborhood. Finally a teacher came who could read the signs of genius. With infinite love and tact, and the whole town against her, she trusted and guided the youth, showing him how to develop his creative powers. He has now modeled wonderful works of art, and bids fair to become a great sculptor or painter. Many a genius is condemned to the prison or asylum for want of a little sympathy from one who understands.

There are in us all certain elements of genius. And we cannot be fair to ourselves and our neighbors, without knowing something of the nature, laws, methods and manifestations of genius. This knowledge enables us rightly to judge and stimulate the masses, judge and emulate the leaders, judge and liberate ourselves. The possessor of unrecognized genius has to fear jealousy, bigotry and lethargy, all due to ignorance. The possessor of recognized genius has to face either enmity or idolatry, both due to ignorance plus imaginary knowledge. Among the foes of genius, idolatry is the worst—the ideals of Emerson and Whitman are most violated by the esoteric primness of the adoring Emersonese and the imitative license of the torrid Whitmaniacs. It is a noble and difficult task always to emulate the greatness of the great but never to imitate their weakness.

Who among your friends is a genius undeveloped? How are you going to help him find himself, reach his place, and carve his name on history? Do you judge men by what they have done, or by what they may do? The small are fascinated by the possessions or the personalities of their friends—the great are fascinated by the possibilities alone. To see limitless expansion ahead of our neighbor, and to want it for him, is to add cubits to our own mental stature.

What now is genius? Merely individuality exalted, intensified, consecrated, educated and employed. The majority of the citizens of this world are copies—not originals. Whereas genius is but the signature of God on a man designed by Himself. If we knew enough, we should say to our boys, "Be as great as the greatest man!"—instead of saying, "Be as good as the best man." For greatness appeals where goodness fails—it is the stream, not the channel, that carries the force.

A recent warfare of words between metaphysicians and psychologists was based on the query, "Can genius be cultivated?" The metaphysicians claimed that every man was a genius in embryo, the psychologists declared that few men could ever attain the heights of poetry, music, invention or finance. The dispute was never settled because neither side had enough genius to prove its case—which might be construed a victory for the negative. The truth is probably this; that a few men and women are born with gigantic brains which enable them to express their highest gifts and immortalize themselves; that all men and women possess talents far in excess of what they use; and that many of those now called irritable, eccentric, perverse, irresponsible, reckless or criminal would become great world-figures if their minds were understood and their powers trained. Genius is not abnormal, it is a flowering of the normal, and whoever does not manifest some form of it is either ungrown or a victim of the blight. As frost on a flower-garden, so is worldly custom on the bloom of genius. Only the very hardy souls can survive the blight—genius might also be called a survival of self against the world.

What is the practical lesson? Just this: Whoever you are, and however circumstanced, you can do and be infinitely more. No matter how friendless, or poor, or sickly, or aged, or unfortunate you may be, some one before you has conquered a worse difficulty or emerged from a greater privation. The path of genius has ever been of thorns —not roses; for roses lure to the valley, while thorns point to the stars.

Study your talents; organize your forces; build an ideal as wide as the world and as endless as God; keep your own counsel; make a systematic study of opportunities leading to your goal; dare to attempt the largest thing in your dream; nurture and guard your vision as most men do their "job"; be your natural self—and laugh at those who laugh at you; form the habit of writing down and preserving all the new ideas or plans that come to you; find the man in history who achieved most nearly what you hope to achieve—then surround yourself with as many books and reminders of him as you can afford to buy; cultivate solitude, the source of inspiration—cultivate friction, the source of development; learn to conserve both time and energy, so that in your leisure hours you can have your genius work; analyze the duties, pleasures and habits that form your daily routine, decide which are non-essential, remove them and substitute real aids to your ambition; believe in your ultimate desire as firmly as you believe in Omnipotence, whence it came; pay the price gladly, in suffering, toiling, starving, waiting, being misunderstood; and measure final success not by the honors of the world nor the clink of gold in your purse, but by your own Herculean effort that builds the Stature of immortality, and by the lightened hearts and illumined souls whose nobler lives praise you with honors everlasting.

For in the end, genius is but the impulse to realize the divine, here and now. Divine beauty, divine strength, divine sweetness, divine skill, divine bravery, divine wholeness, divine love—something divine fills and impels every one who achieves beyond the extent of his neighbors. To grasp this divine leading and be under this divine sway is to attain the impossible, enforce the miraculous, and lift this world onto a level with God.